M000026795

WORKING with Numbers

REFRESHER

COMPUTATION
ALGEBRA
GEOMETRY

STECK-VAUGHN
ELEMENTARY · SECONDARY · ADULT · LIBRARY

A Harcourt Company

www.steck-vaughn.com

Contents

Acknowledgments

Editorial Director: Diane Schnell
Supervising Editor: Donna Montgomery
Editor: Meredith Edgley O'Reilly
Associate Director of Design: Joyce Spicer
Designer: Jim Cauthron
Senior Technical Advisor: Alan Klemp
Editorial Development and Production: Monotype Composition
Media Researcher: Sarah Fraser
Cover Photo: © Chris Tomaidis/Stone

ISBN: 0-7398-4412-1

Working with Numbers provides practice in key mathematics skills and strategies as outlined in the National Council of Teachers of Mathematics *Standards 2000* and in state standards. The program incorporates the goals and concepts of these standards, including mastery of computation, algebra, and geometry skills, the ability to choose and use appropriate problem-solving strategies, thinking and reasoning, and understanding the language of mathematics.

Student Book Features

Clear Presentation of Concepts

A clear and precise explanation of the concept being taught begins each lesson. In the practice exercises that follow, initial problems are solved in a manner that models the presentation of the algorithm or problem-solving strategy. This provides students with an immediate reference when deciding how to solve problems. Each instructional lesson focuses on a single skill or strategy.

The Language of Mathematics

Students are introduced to the language of mathematics in the context of instructional information and sample problems. Lessons provide key vocabulary in mathematics and the different synonyms that may be used. Examples and hints to the students support the meaning of mathematical terms.

Attention to Practice

Every skill lesson includes *Practice* exercises that provide the drill and practice necessary for positive reinforcement of the algorithm. Sample problems are provided to ensure that students understand the concepts before completing the computations on their own. Concepts are practiced and expanded in multiple follow-up lessons, including *Mixed Practice* exercises. Skill practice is broken into several stages of progression to allow students to master rudimentary skills before demonstrating higher levels of application.

Review and Assessment

A *Unit Review* ends each unit and provides exercises similar to those in the lessons. Each student book ends with a comprehensive *Final Review*. Exercises that appear in the *Final Review* parallel those in the *Pretest* and in the *Mastery Test*.

Problem Solving and Reasoning

The *Problem Solving* strategy lessons in each unit provide activities that bridge the mastery of mathematical skills and the application of mathematics in solving real-life problems. Strategies give students tools to explore a variety of ways to solve a given problem. The four problem-solving steps—*Understand, Plan, Solve,* and *Look Back*—provide a logical process for solving problems and encourage students to become better problem solvers.

Teacher's Guide Features

The Teacher's Guides for *Refresher* and *Algebra* include an overview of the program, a scope and sequence chart, teaching strategies and activities for each unit, and a *Mastery Test*. Answer keys for the student books are also included.

Teaching Strategies

Each Teacher's Guide provides suggestions for instruction in unit concepts. For each unit, key vocabulary, objectives, introductory activities, and developmental activities are provided.

Mastery Test

A comprehensive *Mastery Test* is provided in each Teacher's Guide. Each *Mastery Test* parallels the *Pretest* and the *Final Review* in the corresponding student worktext.

Scope and Sequence Chart

The scope and sequence of skills is based on state standards and the National Council of Teachers of Mathematics *Standards 2000*. Skills and problem-solving strategies progress logically and developmentally.

Scope and Sequence

	Refresher	Algebra
Computations, Geometry, And Algebra		
Operations with Whole Numbers, Fractions, Decimals, Integers, and Rational Numbers	•	•
Operations with Irrational Numbers		•
Computations Involving Positive and Negative Numbers	•	•
Ratios, Proportions, and Percents	•	•
Scientific Notation	•	•
Factors and Multiples	•	•
Apply the Use of Variables	•	•
Translate Information Between Diagrams, Models, and Expressions	•	•
Graph Sets of Points in a Rectangular Coordinate Plane	•	•
Work with Applications Using Coordinates	•	•
Solve Linear Equations Using Whole Numbers and Real Numbers	•	•
Solve Inequalities Using Whole Numbers and Real Numbers	•	•
Use Substitution in Expressions and Formulas	•	•
Interpret Systems of Equations and Inequalities Graphically		•
Find Perimeter, Area, and Circumference	•	•
Find Volume and Surface Area	•	•
Measurement	•	
Graph Linear Equations	•	•
Calculate and Graph Slope of a Line	•	•
Understand and Apply the Slope-Intercept Form		•
Understand and Use the Pythagorean Theorem	•	•
Operations with Powers and Roots; Square Root	•	•
Absolute Value	•	•
Understand and Apply the Order of Operations	•	•
Solve Polynomial Equations with Real and Complex Roots		•
Use the Terms to Describe Functions and Their Properties	•	•
Quadratic Equations		•
Distance Formula		•
Problem Solving		
Write a Number Sentence	•	•
Choose an Operation	•	•
Use Guess and Check; Use Estimation	•	•
Make a Drawing or a Model	•	•
Make a Graph, Table, Chart, or List	•	•
Recognize and Extend Patterns and Sequences	•	•
Identify Extra Information	•	•
Work Backwards	•	•
Solve Multi-Step Problems	•	•
Use Logic	•	•
Use a Formula	•	•

Using the Pretest Results

The table below lists the problems in the Pretest and the pages of the book on which the corresponding concepts are taught. After students complete the Pretest, compare missed item numbers to these student book pages.

Item	Page	Item	Page	Item	Page	Item	Page
1a	13	10a	84	22a	152	32b	185
1b	13	10b	80	22b	152	32c	185
1c	13	10c	91	22c	152	33a	187
2a	13	11a	98	22d	152	33b	187
2b	13	11b	98	23a	154	33c	188
3a	12	11c	98	23b	154	33d	188
3b	12	11d	98	24a	155	34a	196
3c	12	12a	99	24b	155	34b	196
3d	12	12b	99	24c	155	34c	196
4a	14	12c	99	24d	155	34d	196
4b	14	12d	99	25a	156	35a	197
4c	14	13a	100	25b	156	35b	197
4d	14	13b	102	25c	156	35c	197
5a	15	13c	112	25d	156	35d	197
5b	21	13d	115	26a	166	36a	216
5c	33	14a	128	26b	166	36b	217
5d	38	14b	128	26c	168	36c	216
6a	16	15a	136	26d	168	37a	216
6b	23	15b	137	27a	160	37b	218
6c	34	16a	137	27b	161	37c	219
6d	41	16b	136	27c	163	38a	220
7a	55	17	78	27d	172	38b	220
7b	55	18	137	28a	162	39a	223
7c	55	19a	138	28b	162	39b	223
7d	55	19b	138	28c	162	39c	223
7e	55	20a	148	28d	162	40	226
8a	56	20b	148	29	180	41	226
8b	56	20c	148	30a	181	42a	229
8c	56	20d	148	30b	181	42b	229
8d	57	21a	150	30c	181	42c	229
9a	74	21b	150	31a	182	43	199
9b	86	21c	151	31b	182	44	203
9c	75	21d	151	32a	185		

Help for At-Risk Students

Working with Numbers, Levels A through F, may be used for students who need instruction and practice in the prerequisite skills necessary for success in *Refresher.* The following chart identifies these skills and the books in which they are taught.

	Level A	Level B	Level C	Level D	Level E	Level F
Computations						
Addition and Subtraction Basic Facts	•	•	•	•		
Addition With and Without Regrouping		•	•	•	•	•
Subtraction With and Without Regrouping		•	•	•	•	•
Multiplication and Division Basic Facts			•	•		
Multiplication With and Without Regrouping			•	•	•	
Division With and Without Regrouping				•	•	•
Computations Using Money		•	•	•	•	•
Fractions: Parts of a Whole, Parts of a Group			•			
Computations with Fractions				•	•	•
Computations with Decimals					•	•
Geometry and Measurement						
Customary and Metric Measurement	•	•	•	•	•	•
Solid and Plane Figures	•	•				
Congruency and Symmetry	•	•				
Perimeter and the Formula for Perimeter		•	•	•	•	•
Points, Lines, and Angles			•	•	•	•
Area and the Formula for Area			•	•	•	•
Volume and the Formula for Volume						•
Pre-Algebra and Algebra						
Properties of Whole Numbers	•	•	•	•	•	•
Number Sentences	•	•	•	•	•	•
Missing Addends	•	•	•	•	•	•
Missing Factors			•	•	•	•
Equivalent Expressions	•	•	•	•	•	•
Input / Output Tables			•	•	•	•
Formulas				•	•	•
Order of Operations	•	•	•	•	•	•
Variables					•	•

The Language of Mathematics

Vocabulary
about how many
addends
digit
estimate
is equal to
is greater than
is less than
periods
place-value chart
regroup
rounded numbers
sum
whole numbers

Building Language
Write two 3-digit whole numbers on the board. Ask students to write three sentences using the numbers and at least one vocabulary word. For example, *398 is less than 402.*

Whole Numbers (Addition and Subtraction) Pages 10–31

Math Skills
Place value; Comparing and ordering numbers; Rounding numbers; Addition and subtraction with and without regrouping; Estimation

Problem-Solving Strategy
Guess and check

Introduction
Write the numbers *3,600* and *360* on the board. Have the students name the place value of the six in each number and tell which number is greater. Then have students find the sum and difference. Explain that students will need to understand place value to complete the operations in this unit and the rest of the book.

Reinforcement Activities
Place Value
Draw a place-value chart on the board with millions, thousands, and ones periods. Highlight each period in a different color. Say the number *2,619,043* and have a student write it in the chart. Repeat with other numbers. Then write *839,715* in the chart and have a student read the number. Repeat with other numbers.

Adding and Subtracting
Materials: number cube, paper, pencils
Have students work in small groups. Toss a number cube six times to generate six digits. The goal of each group is to form two 3-digit numbers that have the greatest sum. Repeat the procedure with a goal of forming two 3-digit numbers that have the greatest difference.

Problem-Solving Activity
Guess and Check
Play *Guess My Number* with the class. Think of a number between 10 and 100 and give two clues for the number. The clues can compare the place values of the digits, give the sum of the digits, or give the difference of the digits. For example, if the number is 53, the clues could be *the sum of the digits is 8*, and *the tens digit is 2 more than the ones digit.*

Assessment
Unit 1 Review, page 31

The Language of Mathematics

Vocabulary
dividend
divisor
factors
product
quotient
remainder
trial quotient

Building Language

Write the multiplication problem *32 × 16* on the board. Have students copy the problem on paper, do the multiplication, and label the *factors* and the *product.*

Write the division problem *325 ÷ 9* on the board. Have students copy the problem on paper, do the division, and label the *quotient, divisor, dividend,* and *remainder.*

Whole Numbers (Multiplication and Division) Pages 32–51

Math Skills
Multiplication and division with and without regrouping; Estimation

Problem-Solving Strategy
Choose an operation

Introduction
Explain how multiplication is like addition. In addition, groups of objects are put together to find the total. When the groups are the same size, there is repeated addition, or multiplication. Have students name some real-life examples of same-size groups, such as pairs of shoes or dozens of eggs. Then ask students to name some real-life situations in which they have shared something equally. Explain that division takes place when a total is separated into equal groups.

Reinforcement Activities
Multiplication
Have students work in pairs. Point out that estimation will tell if the answer is reasonable. Write a multiplication problem on the board. Have one student in each pair estimate the answer while the other student solves the problem. Have students compare their answers and check their work. Write another problem on the board and have students change roles.

Division
Have students use patterns to find quotients mentally. Write the following problems on the board: *42 ÷ 6, 420 ÷ 6, 4,200 ÷ 6, 42,000 ÷ 6, 420 ÷ 60, 4,200 ÷ 60,* and *42,000 ÷ 60.* Have volunteers write the answers and describe the patterns. Repeat with other dividends and divisors.

Problem-Solving Activity
Choose an Operation
Materials: operation cards $+, -, \times, \div$
Give each student a set of operation cards. Then read a problem. Ask students to hold up the operation card that they would use to solve the problem. Then have students solve the problem. If all students do not agree on the same operation, discuss various methods of finding solutions. Encourage students to see if more than one operation can be used to solve a problem.

Assessment
Unit 2 Review,
page 51

The Language of Mathematics

Vocabulary
equivalent fraction
fraction
higher terms
improper fraction
least common
    denominator (LCD)
lowest terms
mixed number
simplify

Building Language
Materials: paper, pencils

Ask students to write two sentences using two different vocabulary words in each sentence. Have the students place a blank where the vocabulary words should be. Then have students exchange sentences with partners and fill in the blanks.

The Meaning and Use of Fractions • Pages 52–73

Math Skills
Understanding, adding, subtracting, and simplifying fractions and mixed numbers; Writing equivalent fractions

Problem-Solving Strategies
Complete a pattern; Make a drawing

Introduction
Materials: one sheet of construction paper per student, scissors, colored pencils
Have students fold their papers in half and then in half again. Ask students to cut along the folds resulting in four equal parts. Ask students to color one of the equal parts. Ask, *How many equal parts are there? How many colored parts are there?* Relate the answers to the definitions of *fraction, numerator,* and *denominator.*

Reinforcement Activities
Equivalent Fractions
Materials: index cards
Have students work in pairs. Have one student in each pair write numbers *1–9* on individual cards and place the cards facedown on a desk. Using a pencil as a fraction bar, have students make a fraction where the first card picked is the numerator and the second card picked is the denominator. Have each pair write three fractions that are equivalent to the one created by the cards.

Practice Finding Least Common Denominators
Materials: index cards
Have students work in pairs using the same index cards from the previous activity. Have each student pick one card and work with a partner to find the least common denominator of the two numbers. Remind students to write a list of multiples for each number first. Have students repeat this process until only one card remains.

Problem-Solving Activities
Complete a Pattern
Materials: index cards, pencils
Divide the class into two teams. Have each member of each team write a number pattern on an index card, leaving a blank for the fifth number. Have the teams switch cards, find the rules, and complete the patterns. The team that correctly completes the most patterns in the least amount of time is the winning team.

Make a Drawing
Materials: construction paper
Write three problems on the board that can be solved by drawing a diagram. For example, *A snail crawls $5\frac{3}{4}$ inches north, $2\frac{1}{2}$ inches east, $6\frac{1}{2}$ inches south, $4\frac{1}{4}$ inches west, and $\frac{3}{4}$ inch north. How far is it from its starting point?* ($1\frac{3}{4}$ in. west) Before class, prepare a diagram for each problem on construction paper. Have students match the correct diagram with each problem.

Assessment
Unit 3 Review,
page 73

Assessment
Unit 4 Review,
page 95

The Language of Mathematics

Vocabulary
cancellation
common factor
invert
reciprocal

Building Language
Write the problem $\frac{3}{4} \times \frac{2}{5}$ on the board. Explain that 2 is a common factor of 2 and 4, then show how cancellation is done. Write the problem $\frac{3}{4} \div \frac{5}{2}$ on the board. Ask students how this problem is similar and how it is different from the multiplication problem. Explain that $\frac{2}{5}$ and $\frac{5}{2}$ are reciprocals because their product can be simplified to 1. Tell students that when dividing fractions, invert the second fraction and multiply.

Multiplication and Division of Fractions
Pages 74–95

Math Skills
Multiplying and dividing fractions and mixed numbers

Problem-Solving Strategies
Write a number sentence; Identify extra information

Introduction
Tell students that you multiply and divide fractions in the same way as you multiply and divide whole numbers. When you multiply, you combine equal groups. When you divide, you separate into equal groups. Write equations such as $5 \div \frac{1}{3} = 15$ and $3 \times \frac{1}{4} = \frac{3}{4}$ on the board. Explain to students that $5 \div \frac{1}{3} = 15$ means that 5 can be separated into 15 groups of $\frac{1}{3}$, and that $3 \times \frac{1}{4} = \frac{3}{4}$ means that 3 groups of $\frac{1}{4}$ is a total of $\frac{3}{4}$.

Reinforcement Activities
Multiplication of Whole Numbers by Fractions
Materials: counters

Students can use counters to multiply a whole number by a fraction. Have students find $\frac{2}{3}$ of 24 using counters. First have students divide 24 into three equal groups. Explain that each group is $\frac{1}{3}$ of 24 and that two groups would be $\frac{2}{3}$ of 24. Have students find the number of counters in two groups. Repeat with other fractions and whole numbers.

Dividing by a Fraction
Materials: fraction strips

Have students work in pairs. Write a division problem on the board, such as $\frac{1}{3} \div \frac{1}{6}$. Direct students to model the divisor and dividend with the fraction strips. Then ask, *how many $\frac{1}{6}$ sections fit into the $\frac{1}{3}$ model?*

Problem-Solving Activities
Write a Number Sentence
Materials: index cards, paper, pencils
Divide students into small groups. Distribute index cards to each group with the following sets of words on each index card: *How many in all? How many more? What is the total?* Ask students to write a word problem that would end with each set of words. Then have the groups trade word problems and solve them.

Identify Extra Information
Materials: newspapers, magazines, index cards, pencils
Have each student cut out a paragraph from a magazine or newspaper that contains numbers. Have students write math questions that can be answered by the information given in the paragraphs. Have students trade paragraphs and questions with partners. Ask partners to identify the extra information by crossing it out.

The Language of Mathematics

Vocabulary
decimal
decimal point
is equal to
is greater than
is less than
multiplier
power of ten

Building Language
Materials: index cards, pencils

Have students write a vocabulary word on one side of each index card and show an example on the other side of each card. Tell students that they may need to highlight or draw an arrow to the example.

Working with Decimals • Pages 96–125

Math Skills
Reading and writing decimals; Comparing and ordering decimals; Adding, subtracting, multiplying, and dividing decimals; Fraction and decimal equivalents; Estimation

Problem-Solving Strategies
Work backwards; Use estimation

Introduction
Write the decimal *123.456* on the board. Point out the following:
- the decimal point separates the whole number from the decimal part
- the place values to the right of the decimal point are read with *-ths*
- the decimal point is read as *and*.

Have a student tell the value of each digit and read the number aloud.

Reinforcement Activities
Adding and Subtracting Decimals
Materials: place-value charts

Write *7.5 + 0.82 + 1* on the board. Have students write each of the numbers in a place-value chart. Tell them to align the decimal points and use zeros where needed. Repeat with a few addition and subtraction problems.

Multiplying and Dividing Decimals
Materials: index cards, pencils

Have students work in pairs. Ask each student to write three decimals on three index cards. Have students choose two cards each and multiply the decimals. Then have students use a similar process to divide decimals.

Problem-Solving Activities
Work Backwards
Write the following problem on the board: *If I multiply a number by 7 and add 16, I get 72. What is the number?* Have students work backwards to solve the problem. Have students make up their own number problems that can be solved backwards.

Use Estimation
Materials: mail order catalogs, newspaper circulars

Have students work in small groups. Tell each group that they must select at least five items that could be purchased from the catalog or newspaper circular. The goal is to spend close to $100, but not more. Each group should estimate the total cost, then add or subtract items if necessary.

Assessment
Unit 5 Review, page 125

The Language of Mathematics

Vocabulary
current value
interest
of
part
percent
percent of decrease
percent of increase
principal
rate
simple interest
whole

Building Language
Materials: newspapers, highlighters

Have students look through newspapers to find examples of the vocabulary words. They should be able to find the words in business sections and in advertisements. Have students cut out the examples and highlight the vocabulary words.

Percents • Pages 126–145

Math Skills
Interchanging fractions, decimals, and percents; Computing percents; Simple interest

Problem-Solving Strategies
Use a bar graph; Use a circle graph

Introduction
Ask, *What does the word percent mean?* Point out that percent means per hundred or divided by 100, and that the symbol for percent is %. Explain that 20% is $\frac{20}{100}$ or 0.2.

Reinforcement Activities
Interchanging Fractions, Decimals, and Percents
Materials: 45 index cards, pencils
Make three sets of 15 cards so that the first five cards have a percent on them, the next five cards have the decimal equivalent of each percent, and the last five cards have the fraction equivalent of each percent. Divide the class into three groups. Have students place the cards facedown on a desk to play a game of *Concentration.* A match consists of three equivalent cards.

Percent Problems
Materials: newspapers, magazines, scissors
Have students look through newspapers and magazines to find examples of percent problems such as finding a percent of a number, simple interest, percent of increase, or percent of decrease. Have students copy or cut out the problems and explain the solutions.

Problem-Solving Activities
Use a Bar Graph
Materials: poster boards, markers
Divide students into small groups. Have students in each group decide on a topic for a survey of their classmates. Possible topics could include favorite color, favorite sport, or favorite type of music. After each group has completed a survey, have students make bar graphs showing the results. Then have each group write three questions about its bar graph for other groups to answer. The questions should involve percents and fractions.

Use a Circle Graph
Materials: newspapers, magazines, paper, pencils
Have students look through newspapers and magazines to find circle graphs. Have students identify at least five different pieces of information that can be found by reading each circle graph.

Assessment
Unit 6 Review, page 145

The Language of Mathematics

Vocabulary
absolute value
algebra
algebraic expression
base
coefficient
constant
cubed
evaluate
exponent
integers
irrational numbers
like terms
natural numbers
numerical expression
opposites
order of operations
radical
radicand
raised to the third power
rational numbers
real numbers
scientific notation
set
square root
squared
standard form
term
to the second power
variable
whole numbers

Algebra: Expressions and Equations
Pages 146–177

Math Skills
Understanding numbers and absolute value; Comparing and ordering integers; Adding, subtracting, multiplying, and dividing integers; Evaluating and writing expressions with and without variables; Squares, cubes, and exponents; Scientific notation; Square roots; Solving equations; Exponents in expressions

Problem-Solving Strategy
Use logic

Introduction
Ask students to write the numerical expressions $1 + 9$, $2 + 9$, $3 + 9$, $4 + 9$, and $5 + 9$. Ask, *What varies in each of these numerical expressions?* Tell students that a variable, or symbol, is used in algebra to represent quantities whose values are unknown or may vary. Have students replace the first addend with the variable n and write the algebraic expression $n + 9$. Now ask students to write the equation $n + 9 = 16$. Ask students to determine the value of the variable (7). Tell students that algebraic expressions and equations can involve addition, subtraction, multiplication, and division.

Reinforcement Activities
Adding, Subtracting, Multiplying, and Dividing Integers
Materials: paper, pencils, scissors
Have students work in pairs. Have one student in each pair cut 21 small squares of paper, with numbers $^-10$ to $+10$ on the squares, and place the squares on the desk with the numbers facedown. Have students take turns picking two numbers and finding the sum, the difference, the product, and the quotient. Make sure students realize that because addition and multiplication are commutative, they can find the sum and product in any order. However, subtraction and division are not commutative and the differences and quotients may be different, depending on which number is written first.

Order of Operations
A good mnemonic device to help students remember the order of operations is *Please Excuse My Dear Aunt Sally.* The first letter of each word stands for the order in which operations should be done from left to right when evaluating a numerical expression. *P* stands for *parentheses,* *E* stands for *exponents,* *M* stands for *multiply,* *D* stands for *divide,* *A* stands for *add,* and *S* stands for *subtract.*

Building Language

Materials: paper, pencils

Have students work in pairs. Give each pair a list of ten vocabulary words in one column and an example of each in another column. Have students match each word with its example.

Writing Expressions

Materials: four index cards per student, pencils

Have students work in pairs to write algebraic expressions on index cards, such as $n + 8$. Explain to students that the verbal expression for $n + 8$ is *a number increased by 8.* When students have written an algebraic expression for each operation, have them trade cards and write the corresponding verbal expressions.

Solving Equations

Ask, *What does it mean to solve an equation?* Make sure students understand that they must get the variable alone on one side of the equation. An important concept in solving equations is understanding inverse operations. Ask, *What operation is the inverse of addition? What operation is the inverse of subtraction? What operation is the inverse of multiplication? What operation is the inverse of division?* Be sure students understand that they can use inverse operations to solve equations. Have students describe how they would use inverse operations to solve the following equations: $y + 7 = 20$, $x - 9 = 15$, $5a = 35$, $\frac{2}{3}n = 8$, $3t + 5 = 29$, $2n - 9 = 21$, and $\frac{a}{6} + 1 = 9$.

Problem-Solving Activity

Use Logic

Tell students that it often helps to draw a picture or make a table to organize problems. Ask students to solve the following problem by making a chart. *A vending machine takes quarters, nickels, and dimes. In how many different ways could you deposit 50 cents into the machine?* Repeat with different amounts of money.

Assessment
Unit 7 Review, page 177

The Language of Mathematics

Vocabulary
coordinates
domain
function
horizontal axis (*x*-axis)
inequality
linear equation
linear function
ordered pair
quadrants
range
ratio
relation
slope
solutions
vertical axis (*y*-axis)

Building Language
Materials: paper, pencils

Divide the class into two groups: function/ inequalities and graphs. Have students use the vocabulary words associated with their group in sentences. Some words may be used by both groups.

Algebra: Functions, Graphs, and Inequalities Pages 178–193

Math Skills
Understanding functions, relations, linear functions, slope, and inequalities; Graphing ordered pairs, solutions, and linear functions; Using the slope formula; Solving inequalities involving addition, subtraction, multiplication, and division

Problem-Solving Strategy
Use a line graph

Introduction
Have students brainstorm a list of careers. Then challenge the class to describe how a person doing each job might use functions, graphs, or inequalities. This is an excellent opportunity to answer, *Why do we have to learn this?* Explain that some people use functions, graphs, or inequalities every day, such as people in jobs that involve data collection and reports.

Reinforcement Activities
Graphing Ordered Pairs
Materials: graph paper, pencils
Have students work in pairs. Have each student draw a set of *x*- and *y*-axes on graph paper and label the origin. Then have students plot three points on their graphs. Students are to hide their graphs from their partners. Students will give clues about the location of each point without giving away the answers. The partners should try to guess the location of each point with a minimal number of clues. For example: *Clue 1, one of my points is in the 1st quadrant. Clue 2, the sum of the coordinates is 8. Clue 3, the x-coordinate is larger than the y-coordinate.*

Functions
Materials: graph paper, pencils
Write the following sets on the board:
$\{(0, \ ^-7), (1, \ ^-5), (3, \ ^-1), (4, 1), (5, 3)\}$,
$\{(5, 1), (4, 2), (^-3, 1), (2, 8), (0, 2)\}$, and
$\{(^-3, \ ^-6), (^-2, \ ^-3), (^-1, 0), (0, 3), (2, 9)\}$. Have each student graph each set and determine if each set is a function.

Linear Equations
Materials: index cards, graph paper, pencils
Have students work with partners. Ask each partner to write an equation such as $2x + y = 7$ on a card. Ask partners to switch cards and find at least 3 points that satisfy the equation written on the card. Then have each student plot the points on graph paper and draw a straight line through the points.

Slope

Materials: graph paper, pencils

Have students work in pairs. Ask each student to plot two points on a coordinate grid and draw a straight line through them. Then have students trade papers with their partners and find the slope of the line drawn by their partners.

Inequalities

Write any inequality such as $7 > {}^-3$ on the board. Have students add 1 to both sides and ask, *Is it true?* Have students multiply both sides by 3 and ask, *Is it true?* Have students divide both sides by $^-2$ and ask, *Is it true?* Generalize the property that when both sides of an inequality are added, subtracted, multiplied, or divided by a positive number, the order of the inequality remains the same. However, when both sides of an inequality are multiplied or divided by a negative number, the sign of the inequality must be reversed.

Solving Inequalities

Have students work in small groups. Have each student write two inequalities with different operations. For example, $x + 5 > 19$ and $28 - y \le 20$. Then have students solve the inequalities written by their groups. Have students check their solutions and discuss different possible methods of solving the inequalities.

Problem-Solving Activity
Use a Line Graph

Materials: newspapers, magazines, poster board, colored pencils

Have students work in small groups. Tell each group to look through newspapers and magazines for a line graph. Have each group draw a line graph on poster board and make up some questions about it. Have each group present its line graph to the class, and have the class answer the questions.

Assessment
Unit 8 Review,
page 193

The Language of Mathematics

Vocabulary

acute angle, acute triangle, angle, area, base, circumference, cubic, degrees, diameter, dimensions, equilateral triangle, face, height, hexagon, intersecting lines, irregular polygon, isosceles triangle, line, line segment, obtuse angle, obtuse triangle, octagon, parallel lines, parallelogram, pentagon, perimeter, perpendicular lines, pi, plane, point, polygon, prism, quadrilateral, radius, ray, regular polygon, right angle, right triangle, scalene triangle, straight angle, surface area, trapezoid, triangle, vertex, volume

Building Language

Materials: poster board, markers

Write each of the following categories at the top of a piece of poster board: *Basic terms, Angles, Triangles, Polygons, Area, Circles, Solid figures.* Have students decide which vocabulary words apply to each category. A vocabulary word may be used in more than one category.

Assessment
Unit 9 Review, page 215

Geometry • Pages 194–215

Math Skills

Points, lines, planes, angles, and polygons; Perimeter, area, surface area, volume, and circumference

Problem-Solving Strategies

Make a table; Use a formula

Introduction

Ask, *Do you know where the word geometry comes from? What other words do you know that start with geo? What other words do you know with the letters metr?* Discuss that the word *geometry* comes from two Greek words, *geo* and *metric,* meaning to *measure the earth.* Explain to students that, in this unit, they will learn about measuring and describing the space and objects around them.

Reinforcement Activities

Lines, Angles, and Polygons

Have students look around the classroom to find examples of intersecting lines, parallel lines, perpendicular lines, acute angles, obtuse angles, right angles, straight angles, acute triangles, right triangles, obtuse triangles, and other polygons. If an example cannot be found in the classroom, ask students to draw and label examples.

Formulas for Perimeter and Area

Materials: graph paper, pencils

Have each student draw a triangle, a rectangle, a parallelogram, and a trapezoid on graph paper. Then ask students to find the lengths of the sides of the polygons and the heights for the triangles, parallelograms, and trapezoids. Have students use formulas to find the perimeter and area of each figure. Ask students to check their answers for area by counting the number of squares within each figure. Students may have to estimate the number of squares that are not whole squares.

Circumference of a Circle

Materials: cans, string, rulers

Divide students into small groups. Give each group a different-sized can. Have each group use a piece of string to find the length of the circumference of their can. Then have students measure the length of the diameter of the can. Ask students to divide the length of the circumference by the length of the diameter and round the answer to the nearest hundredth. Ask each group for its results. Discuss that the answer will always be approximately 3.14, the value for π.

Problem-Solving Activities

Make a Table

Draw several polygons on the board. Have each student make a table. Have students copy the polygons from the board into the first column. The first column of the table should be entitled *polygons.* Have students also have columns for the *names of the polygons,* the *number of sides,* and whether the polygon is *regular or irregular.*

Use a Formula

Ask students to recall the formulas they have learned in Unit 9. Have students make a list of all the formulas and include an example for each.

UNIT 10 Teaching Strategies

The Language of Mathematics

Vocabulary
capacity
customary
direct variation
gram
hypotenuse
kilogram
leg
liter
mass
matter
metric
milliliter
proportion
Pythagorean Theorem
ratio
similar

Building Language
Divide the class into equal groups. No group should consist of more than eight students. Each student in the group must define or explain two vocabulary words to the group. No two students should define or explain the same vocabulary word.

Measurement, Ratios, and Proportions
Pages 216–232

Math Skills
Customary length, weight, and capacity; Metric length, mass, and capacity; Ratios; Proportions; Variation; Similar figures; Pythagorean Theorem

Problem-Solving Strategy
Select a strategy

Introduction
Write the words *length, weight,* and *capacity* on the board. Ask students to give examples of items in the classroom whose length, weight, and capacity can be found.

Ask students to write the ratio of boys to girls in the class. Discuss that two equal ratios form a proportion. Then show students how they can check whether two ratios are equal by cross-multiplying.

To introduce students to shapes, sizes, and proportions, ask them to look around the room and point out figures that are the same shape but different sizes.

Reinforcement Activities
Customary Measurement
Materials: paper and pencil
Write the following table on the board and have students copy the table on a sheet of paper with room for five more objects.

Customary Units of Measure			
Object	Length	Weight	Capacity
Book	inches	pounds	X

Have students list five objects and write the units they could use to measure the object. Encourage students to share examples with the class.

Metric Measurement
Materials: centimeter ruler
Have students measure in centimeters the length of various items, such as a pencil, pen, and a sheet of paper. Then have students write the measurements in order from least to greatest. Ask students how the metric system of measurement is related to the lessons on place value of whole numbers and decimals.

Ratios

Have students count the number of desks and chairs in the classroom and write the ratio of desks to chairs. Have students continue writing ratios by comparing other objects in the room.

Proportions

Write a proportion such as $\frac{2}{8} = \frac{3}{12}$ on the board. Explain to students that if $\frac{2}{8} = \frac{3}{12}$ then $2(12) = 3(8)$; $24 = 24$. Tell students that this method, cross-multiplying, is used to check proportions. Point out that if the products are equal, the proportions are equal. Have students check several more proportions by cross-multiplying.

Similar Triangles

Draw two similar triangles on the board and label them *LMN* and *DEF*. Have students tell which are the corresponding sides and the corresponding angles. Point out that corresponding angles are equal.

Pythagorean Theorem

Materials: graph paper, string, pencils

Have students draw on graph paper a right triangle that has legs of 3 and 4 units in length. Ask students to use string to find the number of units in the length of the hypotenuse. Repeat the procedure with right triangles with sides of 6 and 8, 9 and 12, 8 and 15, and 7 and 24. Then check the measurement of each hypotenuse by using the Pythagorean Theorem, $c^2 = a^2 + b^2$, where a and b are legs and c is the measurement of the hypotenuse.

Problem-Solving Activity
Select a Strategy

Have students make a list of all the problem-solving strategies taught in this book. Have them choose one strategy from the list and write a question that can be solved using that strategy. Ask students to trade papers and solve one another's word problems.

Assessment
Unit 10 Review, page 232

Final Review, pages 233–236

Mastery Test

1. What is the value of the 9 in 97,381?

   Ⓐ 9   Ⓑ 900

   Ⓒ 9,000   Ⓓ 90,000

2. Add.   37,424
           + 5,195

   Ⓐ 5,154   Ⓑ 24,619

   Ⓒ 42,619   Ⓓ 46,219

3. Subtract.   6,037
             − 4,163

   Ⓐ 478   Ⓑ 1,478

   Ⓒ 1,874   Ⓓ 10,200

4. Multiply.   393
             × 148

   Ⓐ 58,164   Ⓑ 3

   Ⓒ 59,641   Ⓓ 60,000

5. Divide. $6\overline{)394}$

   Ⓐ 60   Ⓑ 65 r4

   Ⓒ 66 r5   Ⓓ 75 r5

6. Simplify. $\frac{16}{20} =$

   Ⓐ $\frac{4}{10}$ Ⓑ $\frac{9}{10}$

   Ⓒ $\frac{4}{5}$ Ⓓ $\frac{8}{5}$

7. Find the sum. $342 + 847$

   Ⓐ 500   Ⓑ 505

   Ⓒ 1,100   Ⓓ 1,189

8. Find the difference. $27,403 − 475$

   Ⓐ 26,878   Ⓑ 26,928

   Ⓒ 27,927   Ⓓ 62,878

9. Find the product. 32×151

   Ⓐ 5   Ⓑ 4,832

   Ⓒ 27,928   Ⓓ 5,832

10. Find the quotient. $3,913 \div 43$

   Ⓐ 81   Ⓑ 90

   Ⓒ 91   Ⓓ 100

11. Simplify. $\frac{36}{8} =$

   Ⓐ 4.5   Ⓑ 5

   Ⓒ 4   Ⓓ 6

12. Add. $\frac{2}{6}$
           $+ \frac{1}{6}$

   Ⓐ $\frac{1}{6}$ Ⓑ $\frac{1}{2}$

   Ⓒ $\frac{3}{12}$ Ⓓ $\frac{1}{4}$

13. Add. $6\frac{3}{4}$
           $+ 2\frac{5}{8}$

   Ⓐ $8\frac{3}{8}$ Ⓑ $9\frac{11}{8}$

   Ⓒ $9\frac{3}{8}$ Ⓓ $8\frac{1}{4}$

14. Subtract. $\frac{3}{5}$
             $- \frac{3}{10}$

   Ⓐ $\frac{3}{5}$ Ⓑ $\frac{9}{5}$

   Ⓒ $\frac{9}{10}$ Ⓓ $\frac{3}{10}$

Name _____

15. Subtract. $3\frac{1}{3}$
$\qquad -2\frac{3}{4}$

- (A) $7\frac{1}{12}$
- (B) $\frac{7}{12}$
- (C) $1\frac{5}{12}$
- (D) $1\frac{7}{12}$

16. Multiply. $\frac{9}{10} \times \frac{5}{6}$

- (A) $\frac{3}{12}$
- (B) $\frac{3}{4}$
- (C) $\frac{9}{4}$
- (D) $\frac{1}{4}$

17. Multiply. $3\frac{1}{4} \times 12$

- (A) 39
- (B) 40
- (C) $39\frac{1}{2}$
- (D) 41

18. Multiply. $1\frac{1}{5} \times 3\frac{2}{3}$

- (A) $2\frac{3}{5}$
- (B) $5\frac{3}{5}$
- (C) $3\frac{2}{5}$
- (D) $4\frac{2}{5}$

19. Divide. $1\frac{5}{6} \div 2\frac{1}{3}$

- (A) $\frac{11}{14}$
- (B) $4\frac{5}{18}$
- (C) $\frac{14}{11}$
- (D) $\frac{18}{77}$

20. Divide. $2\frac{2}{5} \div \frac{13}{4}$

- (A) $\frac{6}{65}$
- (B) $1\frac{17}{65}$
- (C) $\frac{48}{65}$
- (D) $\frac{65}{77}$

21. Divide. $3\frac{3}{4} \div 4\frac{2}{7}$

- (A) $\frac{7}{8}$
- (B) $\frac{1}{8}$
- (C) $\frac{1}{3}$
- (D) $\frac{5}{8}$

22. Which is seven tenths written as a fraction?

- (A) $\frac{10}{7}$
- (B) $\frac{7}{100}$
- (C) $\frac{100}{7}$
- (D) $\frac{7}{10}$

23. Which is 2.35 written as a mixed number?

- (A) $2\frac{3}{5}$
- (B) $2\frac{7}{20}$
- (C) $2\frac{35}{10}$
- (D) $23\frac{5}{10}$

24. Which is $\frac{4}{1,000}$ written as a decimal?

- (A) 4
- (B) 0.4
- (C) 0.004
- (D) 0.04

25. Add. 83.057
$\qquad + 16.02$

- (A) 990.77
- (B) 99.077
- (C) 9.9077
- (D) 0.99077

26. Subtract. 9.68
$\qquad - 4.19$

- (A) 0.0549
- (B) 54.9
- (C) 5.49
- (D) 549

27. Multiply. 9.25
$\qquad \times 0.14$

- (A) 0.1295
- (B) 12.95
- (C) 129.5
- (D) 1.295

28. Divide. $2.1\overline{)14.28}$

- (A) 680
- (B) 6.8
- (C) 0.68
- (D) 68

Name _____

29. Which is 47% written as a decimal and as a fraction?

    Ⓐ $47.0, \frac{47}{100}$ Ⓑ $0.47, \frac{47}{100}$

    Ⓒ $0.47, 4\frac{7}{10}$ Ⓓ $0.47, 4\frac{7}{10}$

30. What is 20% of 25?

    Ⓐ 15   Ⓑ 20

    Ⓒ 10   Ⓓ 5

31. What percent of 80 is 12?

    Ⓐ 15%   Ⓑ 92%

    Ⓒ 30%   Ⓓ 68%

32. Solve. $|^{-}1| =$

    Ⓐ $^{-}1$ Ⓑ $^{-}3$

    Ⓒ 1   Ⓓ 2

33. Find the simple interest of $275 at 3% for 2 years.

    Ⓐ $16.50   Ⓑ $165

    Ⓒ $8.25   Ⓓ $82.5

34. Compare. $^{-}4$ ___ $^{-}6$

    Ⓐ >   Ⓑ <

    Ⓒ =   Ⓓ not here

35. Add. $^{-}9 + {}^{-}4$

    Ⓐ $^{-}13$ Ⓑ 5

    Ⓒ $^{-}5$ Ⓓ 13

36. Subtract. $11 - {}^{-}6$

    Ⓐ 17   Ⓑ $^{-}17$

    Ⓒ 5   Ⓓ $^{-}5$

37. Multiply. $^{-}6 \times {}^{-}5$

    Ⓐ $^{-}30$ Ⓑ 35

    Ⓒ 30   Ⓓ $^{-}25$

38. Divide. $^{-}54 \div 9$

    Ⓐ 6   Ⓑ 5

    Ⓒ 9   Ⓓ $^{-}6$

39. Solve. $9 \times 5 + 4$

    Ⓐ 49   Ⓑ 9

    Ⓒ 81   Ⓓ 1

40. Solve. $\frac{12 \times 4}{6 + 2}$

    Ⓐ 4   Ⓑ 6

    Ⓒ 5   Ⓓ 7

41. Solve. $\frac{1}{5}(20) + \frac{1}{4}(24)$

    Ⓐ 10   Ⓑ 9

    Ⓒ 4   Ⓓ 5

42. $\frac{15 + 3(2)}{7} =$

    Ⓐ 3   Ⓑ 4

    Ⓒ 5   Ⓓ 6

43. Which is $z \cdot z$ written using exponents?

    Ⓐ 2   Ⓑ $2z$

    Ⓒ 2^z Ⓓ z^2

44. Solve. $(^{-}5^3)$

    Ⓐ $^{-}125$ Ⓑ 15

    Ⓒ 243   Ⓓ 125

Mastery Test

Name _____

45. Which is 0.00379 written in scientific notation?

    Ⓐ 3.79×10^3 Ⓑ 37.9×10^{-4}

    Ⓒ 0.379×10^{-2} Ⓓ 3.79×10^{-3}

46. Solve. $\sqrt{64}$

    Ⓐ 128   Ⓑ 4,096

    Ⓒ 8   Ⓓ 16

47. If $p = 11$, find $\frac{1}{2}(p + 3)$.

    Ⓐ 7   Ⓑ 4

    Ⓒ 28   Ⓓ 8

48. Solve. $5\frac{1}{4} + x = 12$

    Ⓐ $7\frac{1}{4}$ Ⓑ $6\frac{1}{4}$

    Ⓒ $6\frac{3}{4}$ Ⓓ $7\frac{3}{4}$

49. Evaluate $\frac{2bc(-a)}{2b}$ if $a = {}^-1$, $b = 2$, $c = 4$.

    Ⓐ $^-1$ Ⓑ $^-2$

    Ⓒ $^-3$ Ⓓ 4

50. Solve. $x - 18 = 5$

    Ⓐ $x = 23$ Ⓑ $x = 13$

    Ⓒ $x = 90$ Ⓓ $x = {}^-23$

51. Solve. $6x = 48$

    Ⓐ $x = 24$ Ⓑ $x = 288$

    Ⓒ $x = 80$ Ⓓ $x = 8$

52. Solve. $7x - \frac{2}{7} = \frac{5}{7}$

    Ⓐ $x = {}^-7$ Ⓑ $x = 71$

    Ⓒ $x = \frac{1}{7}$ Ⓓ $x = 7$

53. Solve. $3x - 12 = 33 - 2x$

    Ⓐ $x = {}^-4$ Ⓑ $x = {}^-9$

    Ⓒ $x = 9$ Ⓓ $x = 1$

54. Classify this angle.

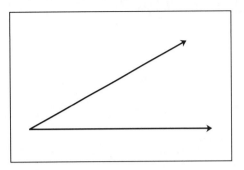

    Ⓐ acute   Ⓑ right

    Ⓒ obtuse   Ⓓ straight

55. Classify this polygon.

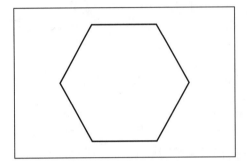

    Ⓐ triangle   Ⓑ pentagon

    Ⓒ octagon   Ⓓ hexagon

56. Classify this triangle.

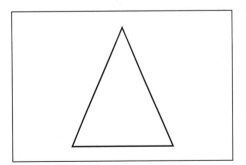

    Ⓐ equilateral   Ⓑ isosceles

    Ⓒ scalene   Ⓓ right

Mastery Test

57. Which of the following is the area of the figure below?

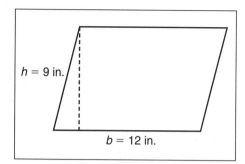

h = 9 in.

b = 12 in.

Ⓐ 42 sq in. Ⓑ 108 in.
Ⓒ 21 sq in. Ⓓ 108 sq in.

58. Which of the following values of y is a solution to: $x + 2y = 5$ when $x = {}^-3$?

Ⓐ $y = 4$ Ⓑ $y = {}^-4$
Ⓒ $y = {}^-2$ Ⓓ $y = {}^-3$

59. Which of the following is the slope of the line that passes through $({}^-4, 1)$, $(1, 6)$?

Ⓐ 1 Ⓑ $\frac{7}{-3}$
Ⓒ $\frac{-3}{7}$ Ⓓ ${}^-1$

60. Solve. $13 + x > 30$

Ⓐ $x < 17$ Ⓑ $x < 34$
Ⓒ $x > 43$ Ⓓ $x > 17$

61. Solve. $7x - 12 \le 16$

Ⓐ $x \le {}^-4$ Ⓑ $x \ge 4$
Ⓒ $x \ge {}^-4$ Ⓓ $x \le 4$

62. Solve. $4 + 3x \ge 14 - 2x$

Ⓐ $x \le {}^-2$ Ⓑ $x \ge 2$
Ⓒ $x \le {}^-3$ Ⓓ $x \ge 3$

63. 64 ounces = ___ pounds

Ⓐ 4 Ⓑ 8
Ⓒ 16 Ⓓ 32

64. 27 inches = ___ feet ___ inches

Ⓐ 24; 3 Ⓑ 2; 3
Ⓒ 3; 24 Ⓓ 3; 2

65. 9 milliliters = ___ liters

Ⓐ 0.009 Ⓑ 0.9
Ⓒ 0.09 Ⓓ 9,000

66. 6 kilograms = ___ grams

Ⓐ 60,000 Ⓑ 6,000
Ⓒ 0.006 Ⓓ 0.6

67. 13 quarts = ___ gallons ___ quarts

Ⓐ 1; 3 Ⓑ 12; 1
Ⓒ 1; 12 Ⓓ 3; 1

68. 6 centimeters = ___ meters

Ⓐ 60 Ⓑ 0.6
Ⓒ 0.06 Ⓓ 600

69. Which of the following shows the ratio of 8 girls to 12 boys?

Ⓐ $\frac{1}{3}$ Ⓑ $\frac{2}{3}$
Ⓒ $\frac{1}{4}$ Ⓓ $\frac{3}{4}$

70. Solve the proportion. $\frac{7}{x} = \frac{49}{63}$

Ⓐ $x = 9$ Ⓑ $x = 8$
Ⓒ $x = 5$ Ⓓ $x = 4$

PRETEST

Page 5

	a	b	c
1.	>	>	<

	a			b		
2.	135	398	516	0.486	40.9	48.6

3. *a.* 8 hundreds

   b. 6 thousands

   c. 4 hundredths

   d. 3 tenths

	a	b	c	d
4.	400	800	800	25,400
5.	1,098	6,611	167,810	15 R3
6.	9,127	49,737	8,808	79 R5

	a	b	c	d	e
7.	$\frac{2}{3}$	$5\frac{3}{5}$	$\frac{1}{7}$	$4\frac{8}{9}$	6

	a	b	c	d
8.	$\frac{3}{4}$	$9\frac{13}{30}$	$1\frac{5}{7}$	$1\frac{1}{2}$

Page 6

	a	b	c
9.	20	$4\frac{4}{7}$	$\frac{2}{3}$
10.	$1\frac{2}{3}$	$8\frac{1}{4}$	$\frac{7}{10}$

	a	b	c	d
11.	$\frac{3}{10}$	$4\frac{13}{20}$	$3\frac{3}{50}$	$\frac{1}{8}$
12.	6.7	2.55	0.16	0.005
13.	4.54	76.67	0.06006	40.1

	a	b
14.	0.08; $\frac{2}{25}$	0.52; $\frac{13}{25}$
15.	40	25%
16.	85	91.2
17.	$301.50	
18.	$8.75	

Page 7

	a	b
19.	$13.13	$36.80

	a	b	c	d
20.	3	2	4	601
21.	⁻2	⁻11	⁻78	19
22.	11	5	50	50

	a	b
23.	$50x$	$z - 17$

	a	b	c	d
24.	⁻11	32	⁻24	7
25.	$x = 29$	$x = 24$	$x = 5$	$x = 9$
26.	$x = 12$	$x = 6$	$x = 13$	$x = 5$
27.	36	⁻8	7	81
28.	3,000	12,000	607,000	890

29. (2, 3) and (⁻4, ⁻3)

Answer Key

Page 8

	a	b	c
30.	$(2, ^-4)$	$(^-1, ^-3\frac{1}{3})$	$(3, 4)$

31. a.

b.

	a	b	c
32.	$^-1$	$\frac{7}{2}$	$\frac{9}{7}$

	a	b	c	d
33.	$x > ^-17$	$x \le 32$	$x \ge ^-15$	$x < ^-8$

	a	b	c	d
34.	scalene	right	equilateral	obtuse
35.	regular	irregular	irregular	regular

Page 9

	a	b	c
36.	3 gal 3 qt	0.04 km	2 lb
37.	3 ft 4 in.	56,000 g	0.334 L

	a	b
38.	$\frac{1}{4}$	$\frac{7}{12}$

	a	b	c
39.	$x = 35$	$x = 30$	$x = 2$

40. XY is 12 feet.

41. MO is 30 feet.

	a	b	c
42.	$b = 4$	$c = 10$	$a = 5$

43. 21 feet

44. 108 square inches

UNIT 1

Page 10

	a	b	c	d	e	f	g	h	i	j
1.	2	3	1	5	6	8	7	4	10	9
2.	7	3	4	11	9	10	2	8	6	5
3.	6	3	7	4	8	5	12	9	11	10
4.	9	13	11	5	6	10	8	4	7	12
5.	8	10	6	14	9	7	12	11	5	13
6.	12	10	6	11	15	8	14	7	13	9
7.	10	8	12	15	11	14	7	16	9	13
8.	8	11	17	10	15	9	14	12	16	13
9.	10	15	13	11	17	9	14	18	12	16

Page 11

	a	b	c	d	e	f	g	h	i
1.	12	13	11	10	15	17	12	15	16
2.	19	15	13	14	13	15	13	19	18
3.	20	18	19	20	20	23	20	22	23
4.	21	22	21	19	21	23	22	21	23
5.	24	19	20	22	22	23	17	22	20

Page 12

	a	b
1.	tens	ten thousands
2.	hundred thousands	millions
3.	5 ten thousands	9 ones
4.	3 millions	4 thousands
5.	645,310	
6.	87,416	
7.	10,089	
8.	eighty thousand, four hundred sixty-two	
9.	five hundred six	
10.	twelve thousand, nine hundred thirty-four	

Page 13

	a	b	c
1.	<	>	<
2.	<	<	>
3.	=	>	<
4.	>	>	>
5.	<	>	=
6.	>	>	>
7.	<	<	>
8.	12	26	34
9.	425	523	643
10.	247	338	617
11.	133	245	873
12.	71	107	170
13.	335	683	836
14.	134	538	647
15.	384	700	916
16.	3,871	4,266	7,109

Page 14

	a	b	c	d
1.	60	80	50	40
2.	30	60	80	50
3.	30	90	20	100
4.	500	700	900	400
5.	800	500	300	200
6.	100	500	700	400
7.	2,500	5,500	6,200	3,700
8.	8,800	6,800	3,300	8,600
9.	18,300	44,200	36,700	11,800

Page 15

	a	b	c	d	e
1.	897	794	579	779	399
2.	777	970	937	999	797
3.	7,879	6,799	7,689	8,888	9,699
4.	7,618	5,899	9,899	9,969	7,378
5.	4,796	9,194	8,899	8,829	7,987
6.	37,787	57,735	68,886	58,788	99,999

Page 16

	a	b	c	d	e
1.	881	581	763	783	591
2.	764	571	882	954	863
3.	673	782	591	764	753
4.	827	508	518	927	756
5.	727	929	439	908	937
6.	871	637	827	884	454

Page 17

	a	b	c	d	e
1.	930	821	737	1,220	1,049
2.	602	1,016	658	202	1,372
3.	3,673	7,822	7,804	5,902	23,176
4.	796	381	5,534	10,590	23,024

	a	b	c
5.	1,025	6,636	10,340
6.	6,060	10,905	6,375

Answer Key

Page 18

	a	b	c	d
1.	800	800	600	600
2.	1,100	800	700	900
3.	1,000	1,200	1,000	1,000
4.	1,600	1,400	900	700
5.	2,000	2,700	3,200	4,400

Page 19

	a	b	c	d	e
1.	924	862	1,333	862	1,528
2.	1,211	1,303	1,352	1,303	657
3.	887	1,505	1,042	899	1,742
4.	8,613	9,188	10,988	7,406	5,800
5.	12,453	4,821	7,569	6,191	12,001
6.	8,583	15,306	8,639	6,025	4,001

	a	b	c
7.	1,049	689	6,584
8.	4,853	7,003	7,180
9.	9,876	9,029	10,201

Page 20

	a	b	c	d	e	f	g	h	i	j
1.	5	4	4	1	9	4	3	2	5	3
2.	9	4	7	2	9	7	0	5	2	1
3.	7	2	7	3	2	6	3	2	4	8
4.	3	0	9	8	7	1	4	1	4	6
5.	7	8	9	7	8	9	6	8	9	7
6.	6	4	8	6	9	5	2	3	2	1
7.	9	7	6	3	4	1	6	4	3	8
8.	6	0	5	0	0	3	0	9	5	5
9.	5	2	0	1	3	5	1	8	2	8

Page 21

	a	b	c	d	e
1.	13	43	10	61	22
2.	62	64	81	83	51
3.	24	48	65	55	61
4.	27	17	10	50	51
5.	112	534	233	411	126
6.	222	132	403	335	304

Page 22

	a	b	c	d	e
1.	233	110	513	450	448
2.	365	10	317	531	116
3.	5,223	6,432	1,520	3,151	1,636
4.	2,071	1,153	3,153	1,230	2,110
5.	161	2,203	1,260	1,200	1,140
6.	2,313	1,115	2,439	4,535	10

Page 23

	a	b	c	d	e
1.	38	44	27	74	32
2.	52	26	17	46	48
3.	47	38	47	59	39
4.	29	19	48	26	77
5.	42	37	32	71	35
6.	48	42	49	32	81

Page 24

	a	b	c	d	e
1.	277	363	661	81	154
2.	792	197	80	495	486
3.	558	181	280	699	132
4.	266	23	150	481	272
5.	190	215	781	205	345
6.	555	91	761	475	141

Page 25

	a	b	c	d	e
1.	359	188	189	266	265
2.	99	267	327	647	86
3.	83	398	578	186	79
4.	473	245	383	273	237

	a	b	c
5.	599	199	472

Page 26

	a	b	c	d
1.	300	300	200	100
2.	500	200	200	300
3.	100	600	0	100
4.	400	700	1,700	1,700
5.	2,000	1,700	4,000	2,300

Page 27

	a	b	c	d	e
1.	117	85	777	963	1,042
2.	45	55	334	335	264
3.	9,898	13,838	6,493	15,713	6,691
4.	6,223	3,217	3,737	6,232	3,573
5.	939	2,183	2,185	1,663	9,999
6.	12,241	33,427	22,166	34,850	77,458
7.	68,799	160,331	31,252	98,899	114,000

	a	b
8.	21,070	742,500

Page 29

1. Earl is 17, and Denise is 25.
2. 58 and 65
3. Jupiter has 16 moons, and Saturn has 18 moons.
4. Five 3-point and eleven 2-point.
5. Five minutes
6. 130 dB

Page 30

1. thirty-five thousand, eight hundred fourteen
2. two hundred eighty-one million, four hundred twenty-one thousand, nine hundred
3. 1,056
4. 100,800
5. fifty-six thousand, nine hundred forty-six
6. four thousand, four hundred
7. 1903
8. 5,526 miles
9. 29,035 feet
10. 8 red balls

Page 31   Unit 1 Review

	a	b	c	d	
1.	400	8,800	500	4,600	

	a	b	c	d	e
2.	77	57	78	84	489
3.	747	918	752	1,104	10,223
4.	23	45	36	57	56
5.	523	306	294	558	3,461

6. 29,510 days
7. 18 years old and 20 years old

Unit 2

Page 32

	a	b	c	d	e	f	g	h	i	j
1.	5	24	0	2	9	28	12	0	30	0
2.	27	32	35	2	45	7	0	25	14	8
3.	49	10	42	24	12	24	18	18	12	32
4.	3	0	18	24	56	6	36	7	16	18
5.	14	72	36	21	48	72	30	64	63	28
6.	12	20	56	42	81	10	6	27	8	3
7.	54	63	54	21	4	9	36	8	15	40
8.	48	0	15	0	0	9	0	6	45	35
9.	40	16	5	1	6	20	4	8	4	16

Page 33

	a	b	c	d	e
1.	48	96	147	208	48
2.	144	299	882	671	528
3.	176	861	121	726	736

Page 34

	a	b	c	d	
1.	236	84	351	782	

	a	b	c	d	e
2.	162	100	378	108	136
3.	456	756	672	975	580
4.	768	216	559	651	1,003

Page 35

	a	b	c	d	
1.	1,786	8,544	7,592	16,606	

	a	b	c	d	e
2.	2,166	980	12,644	11,662	4,296
3.	5,504	7,315	7,056	7,350	23,644
4.	28,880	7,644	25,550	33,792	347,655

Answer Key

Page 36

	a	b	c	d	e
1.	693	824	448	996	848
2.	6,152	4,950	7,136	4,347	3,752
3.	6,792	6,075	4,675	4,788	2,592
4.	1,260	1,120	1,470	1,850	250
5.	1,325	2,162	5,220	2,166	448
6.	5,928	5,544	35,144	19,470	9,614

	a	b	c
7.	16,716	34,632	1,704

Page 37

	a	b
1.	3	6
2.	2	5

	a	b	c	d	e	f	g	h	i	j
3.	5	4	0	1	9	4	3	0	5	1
4.	9	4	7	2	9	1	0	5	2	1
5.	7	2	7	3	2	6	3	2	4	8
6.	3	0	9	8	7	1	4	6	4	6
7.	7	8	9	7	8	9	6	8	9	7
8.	6	4	8	6	9	5	2	3	2	0
9.	9	7	6	3	4	1	6	4	3	8
10.	6	0	5	0	7	3	1	0	5	5
11.	5	2	0	1	3	5	1	8	2	8

Page 38

	a	b	c	d
1.	15 R1	28 R2	12 R6	13 R3
2.	38 R3	60	103	26 R1

Page 39

	a	b	c	d	e
1.	23	21 R3	10 R4	10 R2	9 R5
2.	142	121	114 R2	144 R2	34 R2
3.	29 R3	20	31 R5	185 R3	178
4.	16 R4	100 R7	123 R4	62 R6	163

	a	b	c
5.	64	6 R3	70 R3

Mixed Practice

	a	b	c	d
1.	708	4,417	52,939	19,079
2.	3,000	963	14,432	49,932

Page 40

	a	b	c	d
1.	42 R1	22 R2	22 R1	19
2.	61 R1	51 R2	71 R3	258 R1
3.	209	61 R3	31 R3	315 R1

Page 41

	a	b	c	d
1.	22 R3	21 R7	20 R10	204
2.	9 R5	22 R20	4 R24	8 R55
3.	52 R1	113 R39	31 R31	70 R1

Page 42

	a	b	c	d
1.	3 R27	4 R42	5 R10	5 R5
2.	7 R9	7 R48	6 R37	6 R26
3.	3 R79	7 R28	5 R6	6 R4
4.	7 R6	7 R8	9	6 R48
5.	5 R90	6 R9	5 R11	6 R6

Page 43

	a	b	c	d
1.	314	1,294 R16	971	1,075 R45
2.	845 R37	516	1,733 R25	183 R33

Page 44

	a	b	c	d
1.	233 R107	40 R207	14 R13	9 R132
2.	73 R44	82 R872	860	501 R210

Page 45

	a	b	c	d
1.	288	957	15,552	203,200
2.	888	4,368	44,620	618,372
3.	358,812	2,980,055	136,752	2,270,436
4.	13 R15	939 R1	640 R3	5,219
5.	4	213 R25	73 R10	314 R10
6.	847	483 R8	608 R20	126

Answer Key

Page 46

	a	b	c	d
1.	3,200	300	1,800	2,400
2.	2,400	4,800	2,000	2,700
3.	8,000	24,000	12,000	12,000
4.	350,000	180,000	240,000	280,000

	a	b	c
5.	2,800	9,000	140,000
6.	720,000	12,000	1,200

Page 47

	a	b	c
1.	90	80	50
2.	600	800	400
3.	20	20	30
4.	70	20	15
5.	10	18	16

Page 49

1. addition; 2,089 miles
2. multiplication; 405 hours
3. subtraction; 87,427 miles
4. subtraction; 1,578 strikeouts
5. multiplication; 280 miles
6. multiplication; 720 days
7. addition; the year 2062
8. division; 7 pints

Page 50

1. 19 gallons
2. 432 people
3. $1,000
4. 216 feet
5. 3 miles a day; 84 miles in 4 weeks
6. $520
7. 28 teams
8. about 12,000 gallons

Page 51   Unit 2 Review

	a	b	c	d
1.	400	2,000	100	40
2.	2,550	9,228	1,426	2,668
3.	13,480	57,204	126,763	170,856
4.	173	446 R4	4,218	3 R13
5.	232 R31	117 R8	2,314 R11	315 R46

6. 2,268 miles
7. 425 miles per hour

UNIT 3

Page 52

1. a. $\frac{2}{6}$ or two sixths
   b. $\frac{5}{10}$ or five tenths
   c. $\frac{3}{8}$ or three eighths

	a	b	c
2.	$\frac{3}{5}$	$\frac{2}{3}$	$\frac{5}{8}$
3.	$\frac{1}{6}$	$\frac{9}{9}$	$\frac{4}{7}$
4.	$\frac{7}{10}$	$\frac{1}{8}$	$\frac{1}{2}$

5. a. Two sevenths
   b. Six sixths
   c. Three tenths
6. a. Eight ninths
   b. Four fifths
   c. Seven eighths
7. a. One fifth
   b. Three sevenths
   c. One third

Page 53

	a	b	c	d
1.	4	3	2	1
2.	$1\frac{1}{12}$	$1\frac{1}{2}$	$1\frac{1}{3}$	$1\frac{1}{4}$
3.	$1\frac{3}{8}$	6	$1\frac{3}{4}$	3
4.	16	$2\frac{1}{5}$	2	$4\frac{1}{6}$
5.	$\frac{9}{2}$	$\frac{29}{5}$	$\frac{20}{3}$	$\frac{29}{4}$
6.	$\frac{27}{10}$	$\frac{74}{9}$	$\frac{88}{5}$	$\frac{77}{8}$

Answer Key

Page 54

	a	b	c	d
1.	$\frac{6}{9}$	$\frac{15}{30}$	$\frac{9}{12}$	$\frac{6}{15}$
2.	$\frac{7}{14}$	$\frac{15}{18}$	$\frac{8}{10}$	$\frac{6}{16}$
3.	$\frac{9}{12}$	$\frac{5}{15}$	$\frac{8}{20}$	$\frac{20}{24}$
	$\frac{2}{12}$	$\frac{12}{15}$	$\frac{5}{20}$	$\frac{21}{24}$
4.	$\frac{14}{21}$	$\frac{18}{20}$	$\frac{5}{10}$	$\frac{2}{6}$
	$\frac{15}{21}$	$\frac{15}{20}$	$\frac{6}{10}$	$\frac{3}{6}$

Page 55

	a	b	c	d
1.	$\frac{3}{4}$	$\frac{1}{2}$	$\frac{1}{3}$	$\frac{3}{4}$
2.	$\frac{5}{6}$	$\frac{2}{5}$	$\frac{1}{4}$	$\frac{2}{3}$
3.	$\frac{1}{3}$	$\frac{7}{8}$	$\frac{1}{2}$	$\frac{2}{5}$
4.	$\frac{1}{2}$	$\frac{2}{3}$	$\frac{1}{3}$	$\frac{1}{5}$
5.	$\frac{2}{3}$	$\frac{1}{3}$	$\frac{1}{5}$	$\frac{3}{7}$
6.	$\frac{4}{7}$	$\frac{1}{6}$	$\frac{3}{5}$	$\frac{1}{3}$

Page 56

	a	b	c	d	e
1.	$\frac{1}{2}$	$\frac{3}{5}$	$\frac{1}{3}$	1	$\frac{4}{5}$
2.	$1\frac{1}{5}$	$\frac{7}{8}$	$1\frac{1}{3}$	1	$\frac{10}{11}$
3.	$\frac{1}{2}$	$\frac{1}{5}$	$\frac{1}{5}$	$\frac{1}{2}$	$\frac{4}{5}$

Page 57

	a	b	c	d
1.	$1\frac{1}{3}$	$\frac{7}{8}$	$\frac{7}{8}$	$1\frac{1}{8}$
2.	$1\frac{4}{9}$	$\frac{8}{9}$	$\frac{1}{2}$	$\frac{6}{7}$
3.	$1\frac{2}{15}$	1	$\frac{11}{14}$	$\frac{3}{4}$

	a	b	c
4.	$1\frac{1}{10}$	$1\frac{7}{16}$	$\frac{2}{3}$

Page 58

	a	b	c	d
1.	$1\frac{5}{18}$	$1\frac{7}{15}$	$\frac{19}{30}$	$\frac{13}{14}$
2.	$1\frac{5}{12}$	$1\frac{13}{30}$	$\frac{19}{28}$	$\frac{3}{4}$
3.	$1\frac{8}{45}$	$1\frac{24}{55}$	$1\frac{13}{24}$	$\frac{29}{56}$

	a	b	c
4.	$1\frac{5}{24}$	$1\frac{7}{12}$	$\frac{20}{21}$

Page 59

	a	b	c	d
1.	$5\frac{1}{2}$	$2\frac{1}{2}$	$3\frac{5}{14}$	$9\frac{2}{3}$
2.	$15\frac{7}{9}$	$5\frac{3}{8}$	$5\frac{7}{8}$	$9\frac{3}{5}$
3.	$8\frac{39}{56}$	$6\frac{7}{12}$	$9\frac{9}{10}$	$19\frac{19}{20}$
4.	$7\frac{3}{5}$	$4\frac{11}{12}$	$10\frac{13}{24}$	$15\frac{9}{10}$

Page 61

1. $\$61\frac{1}{2}$
2. 2,060 km
3. Add $1\frac{1}{3}$; 14
4. Multiply by 3; 405, 1,215
5. Add $\frac{5}{8}$; $3\frac{1}{2}$
6. Divide by 4; 80
7. Add $\$1,780$; $\$43,600$
8. Add $\frac{1}{4}$ inch; $4\frac{1}{2}$ inches

Page 62

	a	b	c
1.	$4\frac{5}{12}$	$10\frac{7}{12}$	$3\frac{39}{88}$
2.	$10\frac{17}{56}$	$11\frac{1}{3}$	$11\frac{5}{9}$
3.	$6\frac{1}{6}$	$9\frac{1}{18}$	$8\frac{5}{12}$
4.	$5\frac{1}{2}$	$14\frac{4}{5}$	$9\frac{5}{12}$

Page 63

1. $\frac{2}{3}$ of the residents
2. $\frac{1}{5}$ mile farther
3. 62 feet of rope
4. $23\frac{9}{16}$ pounds total
5. $44\frac{1}{3}$ yards left
6. $2\frac{1}{4}$ ounces total
7. $127\frac{19}{20}$ inches total
8. $64\frac{7}{10}$ cm total

Page 64

	a	b	c	d
1.	$\frac{1}{5}$	$\frac{1}{6}$	$\frac{5}{16}$	$\frac{1}{20}$
2.	$\frac{19}{70}$	$\frac{1}{12}$	$\frac{1}{10}$	$\frac{5}{12}$
3.	$\frac{11}{35}$	$\frac{23}{40}$	$\frac{1}{12}$	$\frac{5}{8}$
4.	$\frac{7}{24}$	$\frac{1}{2}$	$\frac{2}{15}$	$\frac{1}{10}$

Page 65

	a	b	c	d
1.	$\frac{1}{24}$	$\frac{19}{36}$	$\frac{11}{24}$	$\frac{12}{55}$
2.	$\frac{3}{10}$	$\frac{37}{72}$	$\frac{1}{2}$	$\frac{3}{5}$
3.	$\frac{7}{12}$	$\frac{5}{18}$	$\frac{3}{14}$	$\frac{3}{8}$

	a	b	c
4.	$\frac{13}{24}$	$\frac{5}{8}$	$\frac{3}{10}$

Mixed Practice

	a	b	c	d
1.	11,036	31,391	$13\frac{5}{12}$	$10\frac{7}{10}$
2.	741	7,314	1,110	79 R21

Page 66

	a	b	c	d
1.	$11\frac{2}{2}$	$2\frac{9}{9}$	$20\frac{10}{10}$	$41\frac{24}{24}$
2.	$6\frac{5}{5}$	$13\frac{7}{7}$	$15\frac{11}{11}$	$34\frac{6}{6}$
3.	$7\frac{3}{5}$	$4\frac{1}{4}$	$2\frac{1}{6}$	$1\frac{2}{3}$
4.	$7\frac{6}{11}$	$1\frac{1}{3}$	$7\frac{5}{7}$	$5\frac{1}{6}$
5.	$7\frac{2}{3}$	$1\frac{2}{5}$	$4\frac{1}{2}$	$2\frac{3}{4}$

Page 67

	a	b	c	d
1.	$5\frac{1}{6}$	$1\frac{5}{7}$	$6\frac{5}{6}$	$12\frac{2}{7}$
2.	$3\frac{5}{9}$	$3\frac{3}{4}$	$17\frac{8}{9}$	$2\frac{7}{16}$
3.	$5\frac{1}{6}$	$11\frac{2}{3}$	$1\frac{5}{8}$	$2\frac{3}{5}$
4.	$\frac{3}{10}$	$2\frac{4}{5}$	$7\frac{2}{5}$	$4\frac{3}{8}$

	a	b	c
5.	$9\frac{1}{4}$	$5\frac{4}{5}$	$6\frac{5}{12}$
6.	$2\frac{4}{9}$	$1\frac{1}{2}$	$8\frac{7}{10}$

Mixed Practice

	a	b	c	d
1.	104 R20	2,185,556	256	1,682,862

Page 68

	a	b	c
1.	$8\frac{5}{4}$	$2\frac{7}{5}$	$11\frac{9}{8}$
2.	$4\frac{4}{3}$	$5\frac{10}{7}$	$6\frac{11}{6}$
3.	$3\frac{1}{2}$	$2\frac{2}{3}$	$2\frac{3}{5}$
4.	$5\frac{4}{9}$	$1\frac{5}{8}$	$5\frac{3}{4}$
5.	$3\frac{7}{36}$	$2\frac{5}{12}$	$4\frac{7}{24}$

Page 69

	a	b	c
1.	$1\frac{2}{5}$	$1\frac{2}{3}$	$6\frac{9}{10}$
2.	$2\frac{1}{2}$	$2\frac{5}{12}$	$5\frac{23}{28}$
3.	$3\frac{27}{40}$	$1\frac{2}{3}$	$14\frac{3}{8}$
4.	$12\frac{7}{8}$	$5\frac{7}{8}$	$7\frac{1}{18}$
5.	$1\frac{1}{4}$	$2\frac{1}{6}$	$5\frac{23}{40}$

Mixed Practice

	a	b	c	d
1.	1,100	22,000	21,100	6,000

Page 71

1. $18\frac{1}{4}$ feet
2. Ted, David, Shawna, Ellen, Carlos
3. Sam will have picked more.
4. 8,364 feet below the cloud
5. $\frac{3}{4}$ mile
6. $1\frac{3}{4}$ inches

Page 72

1. $\frac{3}{10}$ did not use a computer.
2. $2\frac{1}{2}$ inches
3. Bentley stock is $\frac{3}{8}$ dollar less.
4. $4\frac{3}{4}$ pounds
5. $199\frac{5}{6}$ carat difference
6. $3\frac{3}{4}$ miles from town
7. $3\frac{1}{5}$ inches of rain
8. $6\frac{1}{4}$ inches

Page 73   Unit 3 Review

	a	b	c	d
1.	$\frac{13}{3}$	$\frac{17}{3}$	$\frac{32}{5}$	$\frac{69}{8}$
2.	$5\frac{2}{3}$	$4\frac{3}{4}$	$6\frac{1}{5}$	$5\frac{2}{9}$
3.	3	$2\frac{2}{9}$	3	$5\frac{1}{5}$
4.	$\frac{6}{9}$	$\frac{12}{16}$	$\frac{28}{35}$	$\frac{14}{20}$
5.	1	1	$1\frac{2}{5}$	$1\frac{2}{3}$
6.	$1\frac{17}{30}$	$9\frac{7}{20}$	$\frac{2}{5}$	$9\frac{3}{5}$
7.	$1\frac{3}{8}$	$5\frac{14}{15}$	$\frac{3}{4}$	$6\frac{13}{20}$

8. $1\frac{1}{12}$ yards
9. $8\frac{13}{20}$ miles

Answer Key

UNIT 4

Page 74

	a	b
1.	$\frac{8}{15}$	$\frac{8}{35}$
2.	$\frac{1}{6}$	$\frac{2}{15}$
3.	$\frac{21}{32}$	$\frac{16}{45}$
4.	$\frac{2}{5}$	$\frac{3}{16}$
5.	$\frac{1}{3}$	$\frac{2}{15}$
6.	$\frac{2}{7}$	$\frac{1}{3}$
7.	$\frac{1}{6}$	$\frac{1}{4}$

Page 75

	a	b
1.	$\frac{2}{35}$	$\frac{3}{56}$
2.	$\frac{3}{5}$	$\frac{4}{7}$
3.	$\frac{7}{22}$	$\frac{1}{10}$
4.	$\frac{1}{7}$	$\frac{6}{13}$
5.	$\frac{1}{6}$	$\frac{2}{3}$
6.	$\frac{1}{6}$	$\frac{1}{4}$
7.	$\frac{1}{9}$	$\frac{1}{3}$
8.	$\frac{1}{6}$	$\frac{1}{4}$

Page 76

	a	b	c	d
1.	$\frac{1}{1}$	$\frac{27}{1}$	$\frac{19}{1}$	$\frac{52}{1}$
2.	$\frac{7}{1}$	$\frac{36}{1}$	$\frac{125}{1}$	$\frac{11}{1}$

	a	b
3.	15	8
4.	10	$2\frac{2}{3}$
5.	50	15
6.	9	$13\frac{1}{2}$
7.	5	9
8.	$6\frac{3}{4}$	4

Page 77

	a	b
1.	$4\frac{4}{5}$	7
2.	15	$3\frac{1}{2}$
3.	30	6
4.	$2\frac{2}{3}$	15
5.	11	3
6.	25	25
7.	$\frac{4}{7}$	12
8.	15	9

Mixed Practice

	a	b	c	d
1.	5,656	466	16,209	5,866
2.	12,673	41	31,863	8,894

Page 78

	a	b
1.	6	$14\frac{1}{4}$
2.	21	9
3.	$7\frac{13}{15}$	$100\frac{1}{10}$
4.	242	$43\frac{1}{2}$
5.	10	$25\frac{3}{7}$
6.	$4\frac{9}{10}$	$16\frac{1}{10}$
7.	$19\frac{1}{4}$	$10\frac{1}{3}$
8.	$27\frac{1}{2}$	$5\frac{1}{2}$

Page 79

	a	b		a	b
1.	$1\frac{3}{4}$	2	2.	$3\frac{1}{2}$	1
3.	$\frac{4}{5}$	$1\frac{3}{4}$	4.	3	$1\frac{1}{2}$
5.	$1\frac{5}{16}$	$\frac{1}{2}$	6.	$3\frac{5}{6}$	2
7.	$\frac{5}{6}$	$1\frac{3}{16}$	8.	2	$2\frac{3}{16}$

Page 80

	a	b		a	b
1.	$5\frac{13}{24}$	$3\frac{1}{3}$	2.	$10\frac{4}{5}$	$4\frac{19}{20}$
3.	$1\frac{7}{8}$	10	4.	10	$14\frac{7}{16}$
5.	9	$8\frac{2}{3}$	6.	$12\frac{2}{15}$	$6\frac{3}{4}$
7.	$2\frac{1}{5}$	$10\frac{5}{8}$	8.	$3\frac{1}{5}$	$10\frac{11}{15}$

Page 81

1. 12 gallons
2. $14\frac{1}{4}$ cups
3. $\frac{5}{16}$ mile
4. $1\frac{1}{2}$ miles
5. $3\frac{1}{3}$ yards
6. $\frac{3}{16}$ mile
7. $102.00
8. $232\frac{4}{5}$ inches

Page 83

1. 30 feet
2. $24\frac{1}{2}$ cups
3. 250 gallons
4. 32 cars
5. 74 feet
6. $\frac{3}{8}$ mile
7. 10 minutes
8. 10 inches

Page 84

	a	b	c	d	e
1.	$\frac{9}{2}$	$\frac{4}{3}$	$\frac{6}{5}$	$\frac{10}{7}$	$\frac{8}{1}$
2.	$\frac{9}{8}$	$\frac{7}{1}$	$\frac{2}{1}$	$\frac{5}{2}$	$\frac{11}{5}$

	a	b
3.	$\frac{1}{2}$	$1\frac{1}{9}$
4.	$1\frac{1}{4}$	$\frac{2}{3}$
5.	$\frac{2}{3}$	$1\frac{13}{32}$
6.	$5\frac{1}{3}$	$1\frac{1}{2}$
7.	$1\frac{7}{9}$	$1\frac{5}{11}$
8.	$1\frac{1}{5}$	$1\frac{1}{2}$

Page 85

	a	b
1.	$\frac{3}{8}$	$\frac{5}{9}$
2.	$1\frac{1}{2}$	$2\frac{1}{3}$
3.	$2\frac{1}{10}$	$6\frac{2}{3}$
4.	1	$\frac{5}{8}$
5.	$\frac{8}{27}$	2
6.	$\frac{24}{35}$	$\frac{2}{3}$
7.	$1\frac{1}{3}$	$\frac{2}{3}$
8.	2	$1\frac{2}{3}$

Mixed Practice

	a	b	c	d
1.	126,513	22	966	10,915
2.	61,824	531	61,104	118

Page 86

	a	b	c	d	e
1.	$\frac{1}{3}$	$\frac{1}{9}$	$\frac{1}{7}$	$\frac{1}{2}$	$\frac{1}{16}$
2.	$\frac{1}{10}$	$\frac{1}{125}$	$\frac{1}{36}$	$\frac{1}{21}$	$\frac{1}{48}$

	a	b
3.	$\frac{1}{4}$	$\frac{2}{7}$
4.	$\frac{5}{42}$	$\frac{2}{15}$
5.	$\frac{1}{10}$	$\frac{12}{125}$
6.	$\frac{1}{9}$	$\frac{2}{25}$
7.	$\frac{1}{12}$	$\frac{2}{9}$
8.	$\frac{11}{84}$	$\frac{3}{32}$

Page 87

	a	b
1.	$\frac{1}{16}$	$\frac{5}{54}$
2.	$\frac{1}{25}$	$\frac{13}{64}$
3.	$\frac{2}{7}$	$\frac{1}{16}$
4.	$\frac{1}{16}$	$\frac{11}{36}$
5.	$\frac{1}{28}$	$\frac{1}{20}$
6.	$\frac{1}{45}$	$\frac{3}{16}$

Mixed Practice

	a	b	c	d
1.	1,742	593	83,551	20,194
2.	2,303	1,928	22,646	40,185
3.	24	56	32	11

Page 88

	a	b
1.	2	8
2.	8	16
3.	20	48
4.	18	$4\frac{1}{2}$
5.	60	48
6.	36	$9\frac{1}{3}$
7.	6	$3\frac{1}{3}$
8.	12	$1\frac{1}{5}$

Answer Key

Page 89

	a	b
1.	$\frac{1}{2}$	$\frac{1}{3}$
2.	$1\frac{1}{2}$	$\frac{3}{4}$
3.	$1\frac{4}{7}$	$1\frac{3}{8}$
4.	$\frac{2}{3}$	$\frac{3}{7}$
5.	$3\frac{1}{3}$	$\frac{2}{3}$
6.	$\frac{5}{16}$	$\frac{2}{3}$
7.	$\frac{2}{9}$	$2\frac{1}{5}$
8.	$\frac{3}{4}$	$\frac{3}{8}$

Page 90

	a	b
1.	14	2
2.	$2\frac{1}{9}$	$7\frac{1}{2}$
3.	11	$7\frac{3}{4}$
4.	2	$1\frac{1}{2}$
5.	$2\frac{3}{4}$	$2\frac{7}{9}$
6.	$2\frac{7}{10}$	11
7.	$15\frac{3}{4}$	4
8.	6	9

Page 91

	a	b
1.	$\frac{1}{2}$	$1\frac{29}{46}$
2.	$3\frac{2}{3}$	$1\frac{29}{41}$
3.	$3\frac{3}{10}$	$\frac{2}{3}$
4.	$3\frac{1}{33}$	$6\frac{1}{2}$
5.	2	$5\frac{2}{3}$
6.	$3\frac{3}{5}$	$5\frac{1}{3}$
7.	$1\frac{7}{8}$	$\frac{3}{8}$
8.	$2\frac{26}{27}$	$2\frac{2}{3}$

Page 93

In each of the following, any extra information should be crossed out in the text.

1. $145.00
2. $72.00
3. $\frac{1}{2}$ foot, or 6 inches
4. 5 feet
5. $12.00
6. $$1\frac{1}{6}$, or $1.16
7. 2,250 yards
8. 6,982 square miles

Page 94

1. 40 cups
2. 26 T-shirts
3. 48 shingles
4. 4 days
5. $10\frac{2}{3}$ tons
6. 4 pieces
7. 8 batches
8. 7 sets

Page 95   Unit 4 Review

	a	b
1.	$\frac{2}{15}$	$\frac{1}{8}$
2.	$\frac{7}{12}$	$\frac{1}{3}$
3.	4	2
4.	$\frac{40}{43}$	2
5.	$6\frac{2}{3}$	$3\frac{3}{4}$
6.	$2\frac{5}{8}$	$3\frac{7}{9}$
7.	$21\frac{3}{7}$	$\frac{4}{5}$
8.	$5\frac{47}{50}$	$1\frac{1}{6}$
9.	$13\frac{1}{2}$	15
10.	13	1
11.	8 spacers	
12.	4 hours	

Answer Key

UNIT 5

Page 96

	a	b
1.	0.3	0.25
2.	0.015	1.5
3.	10.04	5.055
4.	0.175	

5. five thousandths

6. thirty-nine and three hundred seventy-four thousandths

7. one dollar and twenty-three cents

8. fourteen dollars and eight cents

9. six hundredths

	a	b	c
10.	$9.00	$0.90	$0.09
11.	$0.66	$0.11	$42.00
12.	$110.74		
13.	$2,005.03		
14.	$1.19		

Page 97

	a	b	c
1.	<	<	=
2.	<	>	=
3.	=	=	<
4.	>	>	>
5.	<	>	<
6.	=	<	<

	a	b
7.	$0.675 < 60.80 < 67.5$	$7.026 < 7.230 < 7.260$
8.	$1.025 < 1.1 < 1.20$	$0.034 < 0.304 < 0.34$

Page 98

	a	b	c	d
1.	$\frac{2}{5}$	$\frac{3}{5}$	$\frac{2}{25}$	$\frac{1}{500}$
2.	$\frac{21}{100}$	$\frac{83}{1,000}$	$\frac{901}{1,000}$	$\frac{9}{500}$
3.	$4\frac{1}{2}$	$1\frac{31}{50}$	$10\frac{1}{10}$	$1\frac{11}{40}$
4.	$9\frac{7}{100}$	$38\frac{6}{25}$	$5\frac{23}{50}$	$13\frac{4}{5}$
5.	0.1	0.2	0.5	0.7
6.	0.06	0.8	0.052	0.416
7.	5.6	3.1	7.6	0.65
8.	1.03	5.09	1.643	2.051

Page 99

	a	b	c
1.	0.125	0.4	0.15
2.	0.8	0.34	0.44
3.	0.035	0.32	0.375
4.	6.5	2.15	7.4
5.	6.25	1.38	1.56

	a	b
6.	1.45	2.84
7.	6.12	13.02
8.	19.5	4.875

Page 100

	a	b	c	d
1.	$5.41	$0.59	$16.86	$42.24
2.	0.306	29.228	315.3	54.25
3.	$11.43	37.525	1.603	16.737
4.	72.204	23.294	535.00	99.068

Page 101

	a	b	c	d
1.	9.52	10.345	22.536	20.401
2.	38.662	82.233	88.183	44.739
3.	$23.63	45.475	1.815	22.771
4.	5.755	2.849	8.87	7.901

	a	b
5.	13.1	$24.89
6.	58.2	54.073

Mixed Practice

	a	b	c	d
1.	3,510	8,820	22	225

Answer Key

Page 102

	a	b	c	d
1.	3.136	1.16	5.599	$23.77
2.	3.915	4.75	2.04	1.897
3.	4.242	17.20	0.808	$4.14
4.	3.834	1.112	22.36	10.63

Page 103

	a	b	c	d
1.	5.122	2.158	2.014	0.16
2.	$6.96	$24.50	$79.78	$9,032.30
3.	1.625	1.226	1.089	7.45
4.	3.834	79.78	4.505	1.112

	a	b	c
5.	4.015	2.04	22.26
6.	7.45	4.75	1.089

Mixed Practice

	a	b
1.	0.006	0.12
2.	0.020	0.04
3.	0.9	0.040
4.	3.3	6.008

	a	b	c	d
5.	=	<	>	=
6.	<	>	=	<

Page 105

1. $49.49
2. 30 invitations
3. $12.09
4. 225 miles
5. 7:15 A.M.
6. $13.00

Page 106

1. 7.53 million square miles
2. $43.85
3. 9.06 inches
4. 13.25 pounds
5. 580.9 kilometers
6. 1,485.6 kilometers
7. 635.3 kilometers
8. 698.7 kilometers

Page 107

	a	b	c	d
1.	$13	$34	$221	29
2.	80	$1	4	$0
3.	$4	55	125	22

	a	b	c
4.	10.2	8.2	9.9
5.	20.0	4.1	325.6
6.	29.9	20.5	200.0

Page 108

	a	b	c	d
1.	0.9	0.08	3.55	12.37
2.	10.24	0.19	0.83	1.00
3.	3.761	5.653	10.31	442.96
4.	0.6	9.2	0.19	0.07
5.	0.281	11.9	3.704	6.54
6.	0.2322	0.9283	47.40	6.258

	a	b	c
7.	4.218	16.1357	248.692

Answer Key

Page 109

	a	b	c	d
1.	4.846	11.31	18.337	27.97
2.	16.9594	16.57	45.92	390.44

	a	b
3.	12.174	39.254
4.	8.25	56.85

	a	b	c	d
5.	0.234	21.77	3.828	2.76
6.	11.257	5.7645	4.5008	53.997

	a	b	c
7.	11.486	3.125	6.42
8.	26.9933	0.0266	15.47

Page 110

	a	b	c
1.	5.1	2.16	1.414
2.	0.4	0.840	0.95
3.	0.012	0.06	0.054
4.	134.40	5.940	2,134.40
5.	468.66	2,622.87	116.256

Page 111

	a	b	c	d
1.	1.724	0.252	9.78	11.7
2.	40.8	114.08	16.9	33.8
3.	98.4	21.7	350.0	49.5
4.	76.75	3.936	13.806	487.83

	a	b	c
5.	91.2	28.148	855.65

Mixed Practice

	a	b	c	d
1.	199	202	122 R60	69 R54
2.	102 R10	77 R5	160 R40	114 R6

Page 112

	a	b	c
1.	0.64	0.477	0.38
2.	0.072	0.027	0.0008
3.	0.01288	0.408	0.1557
4.	1.425	4.858	46.2
5.	182.508	16.324	14.6016

Page 113

	a	b	c	d
1.	0.18	0.018	4.9	0.252
2.	0.0032	0.0024	1.096	0.01096
3.	0.0021	0.0165	32.86	14.382

	a	b	c
4.	0.0086	0.07622	53.4432

Mixed Practice

	a	b	c	d
1.	26.355	3.696	20.909	5.197
2.	1.094	0.459	9.09	48.6
3.	$105.02	$471.05	$90.69	$199.01
4.	$9\frac{1}{8}$	$16\frac{1}{2}$	$70\frac{3}{4}$	$6\frac{13}{21}$

Page 114

	a	b	c	d
1.	8.2	$0.69	2.76	0.112
2.	0.04	$1.50	0.203	$3.14
3.	4.16	$4.12	0.018	0.007

	a	b	c
4.	1.5	$0.67	1.4

Page 115

	a	b	c	d
1.	4.8	5.29	0.003	$13.70
2.	29.9	6.2	$81.00	4.5

	a	b	c
3.	2.06	0.7	$46.00

Answer Key

Page 116

	a	b	c	d
1.	160	30	5	$340
2.	150	500	$650	400
3.	$35	26	600	$140

	a	b	c
4.	$15	108	820

Page 117

	a	b	c	d
1.	0.5	$0.30	0.4	$0.75
2.	0.02	0.05	$0.80	0.95
3.	0.25	0.125	0.025	0.6
4.	0.5	0.75	0.004	0.25

Page 118

	a	b	c
1.	75	460	0.7
2.	70	460	7.5
3.	0.05	0.008	0.0125
4.	0.125	0.000125	0.1492
5.	6,200	64.215	6.4215
6.	3,150	4.8	0.00048
7.	0.0375	0.375	3.75
8.	37.5	375	7
9.	71,935	16,147	14,920
10.	2.6178	0.0026178	2,617.8

Page 119

	a	b	c
1.	64	64	120
2.	130	8	78
3.	4	2	11
4.	3	6	25
5.	414	3	128

Page 120

	a	b	c	d
1.	2.4	1.032	30.186	4.7173
2.	36	0.06	0.098	0.008
3.	56.52	0.18	0.06	0.348
4.	2.3	826	26,078	12,483
5.	1.28	18.5	5.9	25.3
6.	2.664	1.12	8.96	934.16

Page 121

	a	b	c	d
1.	123.93	6.888	315.375	4.176
2.	0.084	0.2072	0.0005	0.729
3.	30.52875	0.00441	2.3562	0.003776
4.	0.092	0.017	0.03	0.04
5.	2.54	90.6	93.8	1,250
6.	0.625	20	200	430

Page 123

1. about 2,000 quarters
2. about $4.00
3. about 1 meter
4. about 9 bracelets
5. about $10 per hour, about $15,600 per year
6. about 90 miles
7. about $1,200
8. about $8.00

Page 124

1. $606.30
2. 0.92 meters
3. about $10.00
4. Sam paid $1.24 more per CD.
5. 640.9 kilometers
6. 3.0 meters tall
7. 1,100 pounds
8. $0.17 per brick

Answer Key

Page 125   Unit 5 Review

	a	b	c	d
1.	0.1	0.03	0.2	0.75
2.	0.125	0.625	1.25	2.6
3.	$1\frac{1}{10}$	$1\frac{1}{2}$	$\frac{3}{4}$	$5\frac{1}{2}$
4.	18.82	6.309	1.608	40.317
5.	3.38	0.3168	259.64	0.9996
6.	0.05	36.96	8.4	0.166
7.	0.06	0.12	1,200	6.0

	a	b	c
8.	22.5	225	2,250
9.	3.52	0.186	14,920

UNIT 6

Page 126

	a	b
1.	$\frac{41}{50}$	$\frac{7}{100}$
2.	$\frac{1}{100}$	$1\frac{21}{50}$
3.	$\frac{19}{20}$	$\frac{11}{20}$
4.	$1\frac{9}{100}$	$\frac{73}{100}$
5.	$\frac{49}{50}$	$\frac{3}{25}$
6.	$\frac{1}{25}$	$\frac{11}{25}$
7.	$1\frac{3}{4}$	$\frac{83}{100}$
8.	$\frac{13}{50}$	$1\frac{37}{100}$

Page 127

	a	b	c
1.	30%	8%	45%
2.	91%	56%	149%
3.	73%	67.2%	2%
4.	325%	9%	70%
5.	133.3%	54%	62%
6.	37.5%	40%	70%
7.	21%	31.25%	25%
8.	60%	35%	41.67%

Page 128

1. $\frac{6}{10} = 0.6 = 60\%$
2. $\frac{1}{4} = 0.25 = 25\%$
3. $\frac{1}{5} = 0.2 = 20\%$
4. $\frac{17}{20} = 0.85 = 85\%$
5. $\frac{1}{2} = 0.5 = 50\%$
6. $\frac{3}{4} = 0.75 = 75\%$
7. 37%
8. 0.075
9. 0.1
10. 32%
11. $\frac{3}{20}$
12. 0.625

Page 129

	a	b	c
1.	2.05	5	1.75
2.	9.999	3.2	1.013
3.	4.5	6.09	11
4.	8.07	7.255	1.98
5.	2.1		
6.	1.52		
7.	3.33		
8.	1.35		

Page 130

	a	b	c
1.	0.005	0.0033	0.0025
2.	0.004	0.0041	0.0005
3.	0.0025	0.005	0.004
4.	0.008	0.00625	0.00875
5.	0.009		
6.	0.0064		
7.	0.0055		
8.	0.0045 > 0.00375		

Answer Key

Page 131

1. 20%
2. 75%
3. 0.0725
4. $\frac{9}{25}$
5. 9.75%
6. 15%
7. 0.085
8. 80%

Page 133

1. 25%
2. $\frac{3}{20}$
3. 0.3
4. $\frac{1}{10}$, 0.1, 10%
5. $\frac{1}{5}$, 0.2, 20%
6. 0.5
7. $\frac{2}{5}$
8. 30%

Page 134

	a	b
1.	45	180
2.	96	60
3.	30	180
4.	250	54.45
5.	$237.60	
6.	$65.70	

Page 135

	a	b
1.	4	$\frac{2}{3}$
2.	34	$1\frac{1}{3}$
3.	33	3
4.	$1\frac{1}{5}$	$4\frac{2}{3}$
5.	$22.00	
6.	400 students	

Page 136

	a	b
1.	500%	60%
2.	15%	30%
3.	45%	15%
4.	67%	125%
5.	40%	
6.	45%	
7.	11%	
8.	55%	

Page 137

	a	b
1.	68	125
2.	80	200
3.	55	200
4.	730	160
5.	$40.00	
6.	$3,000.00	
7.	13,000 miles	
8.	40 questions	

Page 138

	a	b
1.	$13.75	$14.63
2.	$144.00	$100.00
3.	$8.25	$36.00
4.	$700.00	$17.00

Page 139

	a	b
1.	$112.45	$3.94
2.	$13.36	$577.80
3.	$79.95	$1,072.00
4.	$58.59	$32.81
5.	$317.52	$33.13
6.	$1,207.50	$2,846.25

Mixed Practice

	a	b	c	d
1.	144.24	$255.60	$25.01	0.63
2.	81,536	55	51,788	295

Page 140

1. 63.6 pounds
2. $7.80
3. $108,972
4. 19,812 students
5. $23,540
6. $24.75

Page 141

1. 475 students
2. $24.00
3. $12,800
4. 69 points
5. 548,800 people
6. $119.38

Page 143

1. $2,520
2. $1,275
3. $7,000
4. $3,600
5. $4,400
6. $8,500

Page 144

1. $99
2. $450
3. 75
4. $860
5. 25% increase
6. $320
7. 20%
8. $320

Page 145   Unit 6 Review

	a	b
1.	$26\% = 0.26 = \frac{13}{50}$	$0.2\% = 0.002 = \frac{1}{500}$
2.	$115\% = 1.15 = 1\frac{3}{20}$	$5\% = 0.05 = \frac{1}{20}$
3.	$\frac{7}{20} = 0.35 = 35\%$	
4.	$\frac{81}{100} = 0.81 = 81\%$	

	a	b
5.	40.5	1.8
6.	15%	200%
7.	30	50

8. $200.00
9. 35%
10. $23.10
11. $1,020.00

UNIT 7

Page 146

1.
   a. $a \times b = b \times a$

   b. $x - x = 0$

   c. $n + n = 2n$

   d. $0 \times m = 0$

2. Answers may vary.

   a. $0 + 3 = 3$

   $0 + 5 = 5$

   $0 + 8 = 8$

   b. $8 \div 2 = 4$

   $10 \div 2 = 5$

   $12 \div 2 = 6$

Page 147

1.
   a. natural, whole, integers, rational

   b. integers, rational number

   c. rational number

2.
   a. rational number

   b. rational number

   c. rational number

Answer Key

Page 148

	a	b	c	d
1.	6	9	8	13
2.	18	3	10	15
3.	7	0	17	22
4.	12	19	11	26
5.	30, $^-$30	14, $^-$14	32, $^-$32	29, $^-$29
6.	21, $^-$21	23, $^-$23	42, $^-$42	99, $^-$99

Page 149

	a	b	c
1.	<	<	>
2.	>	=	<
3.	>	<	>
4.	<	<	>
5.	=	>	=
6.	>	>	<
7.	>	=	>
8.	<	<	>

	a	b
9.	$^-6 < 0 < 7$	$^-9 < ^-5 < 7$
10.	$^-1 < 1 < 11$	$^-21 < 12 < 27$
11.	$^-2 < 3 < 8$	$^-13 < ^-3 < 0$
12.	$^-11 < 4 < 5$	$^-20 < ^-16 < 19$

Page 150

	a	b	c	d
1.	2	$^-10$	2	$^-4$
2.	$^-12$	7	$^-7$	$^-18$
3.	$^-3$	$^-8$	9	13
4.	8	$^-8$	0	$^-4$
5.	$^-7$	$^-4$	$^-5$	$^-19$
6.	0	10	2	$^-10$

Page 151

	a	b	c	d
1.	$^-9$	4	12	$^-42$
2.	27	$^-12$	$^-20$	18
3.	24	$^-24$	30	$^-10$
4.	0	20	21	32
5.	$^-6$	$^-4$	3	$^-6$
6.	4	$^-2$	8	$^-9$
7.	6	$^-7$	0	$^-1$
8.	7	4	9	$^-4$

Page 152

	a	b	c	d
1.	30	7	$^-20$	8
2.	18	2	21	$^-20$
3.	35	$^-12$	30	4
4.	8	20	28	30
5.	10	2	$^-50$	11
6.	3	2	$^-8$	$^-13$

Page 153

	a	b	c	d
1.	9	30	13	16
2.	16	26	16	24
3.	14	5	56	10
4.	3	8	5	$\frac{5}{2}$
5.	1	1	$\frac{1}{2}$	7
6.	1	10	3	4

Page 154

	a	b
1.	$10 + r$	$t - 9$
2.	$7s$	$w \div 3$
3.	$m + 12$	$2hx$
4.	$25 - n$	$p - g$
5.	$24 \div k$	$13 + b$
6.	$c - 7$	$y \div 5$

Page 155

1. *a.* 5 is a coefficient, 9 is a constant

    b. 3 is a coefficient, $^-1$ is a coefficient

    c. 6 is a coefficient, $^-2$ is a coefficient

    d. 10 is a coefficient, $^-7$ is a constant

	a	b	c	d
2.	20	8	36	30
3.	$\frac{1}{4}$	10	3	5
4.	85	25	600	300
5.	7	8	1	40

Page 156

	a	b	c
1.	$x = 3$	$x = 4$	$y = 10$
2.	$m = 8$	$n = 17$	$x = 12$
3.	$x = 21\frac{1}{3}$	$k = 13$	$x = 53$

Page 157

	a	b	c	d
1.	$x = \frac{1}{2}$	$n = 35$	$x = 2\frac{1}{3}$	$x = 3\frac{1}{3}$
2.	$k = 25$	$x = 5\frac{5}{8}$	$m = 1\frac{3}{8}$	$k = 13$
3.	$x = 7\frac{2}{5}$	$k = 11$	$x = \frac{3}{4}$	$x = 52$
4.	$k = 11\frac{2}{3}$	$x = 29$	$x = 87$	$x = 5\frac{1}{8}$
5.	$n = 5$	$n = 2\frac{1}{7}$	$x = 16$	$n = 7\frac{1}{2}$
6.	$x = 68$	$x = 8\frac{3}{5}$	$x = 12$	$x = 98$

Mixed Practice

	a	b	c	d
1.	38,373	12,978	34,992	79 R21
2.	1.311	140	35	$3\frac{17}{20}$

Page 159

1. The number is 73.
2. The cat weighs 9 pounds.
3. Tom is 45 years old.
4. The number is 74.

Page 160

	a	b	c
1.	$(2)^2(3)^2y$	$(4)^2(y)^2z$	$(10)^2(7)^2y$
2.	$7(5)^2a$	$(^-1)(3)^2(b)^2$	$7(6)^2(y)^2$
3.	$(^-1)^2(a)^2$	$15(a)^2$	$2(9)^2(5)^2b$
4.	$^-192$	$^-80$	192

Page 161

	a	b	c	d
1.	4^3	$(^-4)^3$	3^3	$(^-7)^3$
2.	$(1)^3$	$(12)^3$	5^3	$(^-20)^3$
3.	216	$^-8$	343	8,000
4.	$^-1$	0	729	$^-512$

Page 162

1. *a.* 5.6×10^6

    b. 6.04×10^6

    c. 6.7×10^3

    d. 1.013×10^6

2. *a.* 3.3×10^5

    b. 7.16×10^8

    c. 2.021×10^9

    d. 2.07×10^6

3. *a.* 410,000

    b. 599

    c. 110,000

    d. 22,300

4. *a.* 8,900

    b. 50,300,000

    c. 3,120,000,000

    d. 75,000

5. *a.* 101,100

    b. 600,000,000

    c. 31,400

    d. 10

Page 163

1. *a.* $8 \times 8 = 64; \sqrt{64} = 8$

    b. $15 \times 15 = 225; \sqrt{225} = 15$

2. *a.* $1 \times 1 = 1; \sqrt{1} = 1$

    b. $6 \times 6 = 36; \sqrt{36} = 6$

3. *a.* $\sqrt{25} = 5$

    b. $\sqrt{9} = 3$

4. *a.* $\sqrt{100} = 10$

    b. $\sqrt{4} = 2$

5. *a.* $\sqrt{144} = 12$

    b. $\sqrt{16} = 4$

Answer Key

Page 164

	a	b	c
1.	$x = 6$	$x = 12$	$x = 10\frac{4}{5}$
2.	$x = 5$	$x = 67\frac{5}{8}$	$x = 14$
3.	$x = 21$	$x = 7$	$x = 10$

Page 165

	a	b	c
1.	$x = 5$	$x = \frac{1}{2}$	$x = 8$
2.	$x = 2\frac{1}{2}$	$x = 5$	$x = \frac{3}{4}$
3.	$x = 4$	$x = 9$	$x = \frac{1}{5}$
4.	$x = \frac{1}{24}$	$x = \frac{3}{10}$	$x = 4$
5.	$x = 4$	$x = 2\frac{13}{17}$	$x = \frac{1}{7}$
6.	$x = \frac{1}{12}$	$x = 7$	$x = 6$

Mixed Practice

	a	b	c	d
1.	977.181	2.2	$\frac{22}{35}$	$x = 30$
2.	$3\frac{1}{3}$	7,196	2.35	3

Page 166

	a	b	c
1.	$x = 10$	$x = 5$	$x = 2$
2.	$x = 7$	$x = 3$	$x = 2$
3.	$x = 15$	$x = 3$	$x = 3$

Page 167

	a	b	c
1.	$x = 1$	$x = 5$	$x = 4$
2.	$x = 12$	$x = 7$	$x = \frac{3}{4}$
3.	$x = \frac{1}{2}$	$x = 6$	$x = 5$
4.	$x = \frac{3}{14}$	$x = 1$	$x = \frac{1}{15}$
5.	$x = 13$	$x = 9$	$x = 10$
6.	$x = 9$	$x = 2$	$x = 2\frac{1}{3}$

Mixed Practice

	a	b	c
1.	8.5	0.16	2,919
2.	96	0.66	7,148

Page 168

	a	b	c
1.	$x = 6$	$x = 5$	$x = 1$
2.	$x = 2$	$x = 8$	$x = 10$
3.	$x = 2$	$x = 7$	$x = 15$

Page 169

	a	b	c
1.	$x = 10$	$x = 3$	$x = 6$
2.	$x = 17$	$x = 1$	$x = 25$
3.	$x = 5$	$x = 30$	$x = 8$
4.	$x = 10$	$x = 24$	$x = 9$
5.	$x = \frac{2}{7}$	$x = 11$	$x = {}^{-}2$
6.	$x = \frac{1}{2}$	$x = 1\frac{2}{3}$	$x = {}^{-}5$

Mixed Practice

	a	b
1.	$0.45; \frac{9}{20}$	$0.75; \frac{3}{4}$
2.	$0.12; \frac{3}{25}$	$1.2; 1\frac{1}{5}$
3.	$0.10; \frac{1}{10}$	$0.03; \frac{3}{100}$
4.	$0.28; \frac{7}{25}$	$0.35; \frac{7}{20}$

Page 170

1. $n = 28$
2. Arsenio has $105, and Malik has $40.
3. Jerry has $3.20, and Pat has $9.60.
4. $n = 48$

Page 171

1. Elena has $35, and Tori has $7.
2. DeWayne has $35, and Hakeem has $20.
3. 1st package has 50. 2nd package has 30.
4. 1st lot has 75 cars. 2nd lot has 125 cars.
5. Mother is 54, and Ricardo is 18.
6. Father is 58, and Natasha is 20.
7. The three numbers are 30, 60, and 90.
8. The three numbers are 20, 40, and 80.

Answer Key

Page 172

	a	b	c	d
1.	2,352	6,561	32,768	1,280
2.	2,187	240	117,649	65,536
3.	262,144	4,096	16	600
4.	8	1,024	720	8
5.	6,588	32,256	9,765,625	729

Page 173

1. a.   7,812
    b.   100
    c.   4,096
    d.   ⁻531,360

2. a.   7
    b.   625
    c.   4,160
    d.   6,561

3. a.   4
    b.   392
    c.   7,776
    d.   279,936

4. a.   1,000,0000
    b.   4,096
    c.   3,250
    d.   49,152

5. a.   343
    b.   387,420,489
    c.   1,000,000,000
    d.   320

6. a.   7,560
    b.   10
    c.   512
    d.   48

Mixed Practice

	a	b	c	d
1.	45	$x = 3$	$5\frac{11}{15}$	1.38
2.	$\frac{4}{21}$	2.5	$21.60	⁻21

Page 175

1. Charles – Red
    Terry – Blue
    Tony – Green

2. Martin – 119
    Anna – 101
    Julie – 123

3. Raul – 215
    Samantha – 275
    Pablo – 260
    Mateo – 130

4. Vanessa – Volleyball
    Yolanda – Tennis
    Kimberly – Softball
    Nicole – Cheerleading

Page 176

1. 018
2. 512 miles
3. 300 feet
4. 128
5. $173
6. 135
7. 243 free throws
8. 557 people

Answer Key

Page 177   Unit 7 Review

	a	b	c	d
1.	30	0	6	85
2.	⁻5	10	3	8
3.	15	28	4	2

	a	b	c
4.	9^2	z^3	17^2
5.	30	⁻3	$-1\frac{4}{5}$
6.	31	119	⁻32

	a	b	c	d
7.	9,400,000	1,230	570,000	89,000

	a	b	c
8.	3	$y = 8$	$t = 2$
9.	$z = ^-10$	$m = 6$	12
10.	$q = 6$	$x = 144$	$s = 2$

11. The number is 14.

12. $10.75

UNIT 8

Page 178

	a	b
1.	yes	no
2.	yes	yes
3.	domain: {⁻10, ⁻2, 1, 9}	domain: {⁻2, 1, 7}
	range: {⁻1, 3, 4, 5}	range: {⁻3, 6, 8}
4.	domain: {⁻1, 0, 4}	domain: {1, 2, 5}
	range: {⁻6, ⁻5, 0, 9}	range: {⁻2, 1, 9}

Page 179

1. **a.** C (0, ⁻4)

   b. D (⁻1, ⁻3)

   c. E (1, ⁻3)

   d. F (⁻2, 0)

   e. G (2, 0)

2. **a.** H (3, 5)

   b. J (5, 7)

   c. K (⁻5, 7)

   d. L (⁻2, 1)

   e. M (3, ⁻1)

3. **a.**

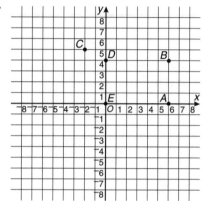

   b.

Page 180

1. (3, ⁻12)

2. (⁻2, 3)

3. {(6, ⁻1), (14, 1)}

4. {(⁻5, 0), (1, ⁻3), (⁻9, 2)}

Page 181

	a	b	c
1.	(‾1, 4)	(‾3, 5)	(5, 1)
2.	(3, 5)	(0, 11)	(‾1, 13)
3.	(‾4, ‾2)	(‾5, ‾1)	(‾9, 3)

Page 182

1.

x	y
0	5
1	3
3	‾1

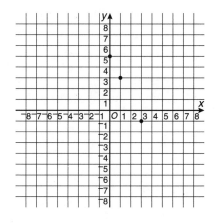

2.

x	y
‾2	‾2
0	‾4
3	‾7

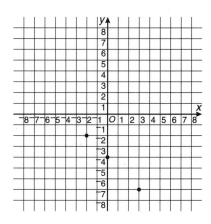

3.

x	y
‾1	‾1
0	2
1	5

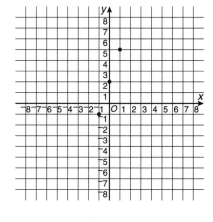

Page 183

Solution points will vary, but line graphs will be the same.

1.

x	y
0	‾2
1	1
2	4

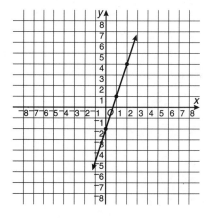

2.

x	y
‾6	0
0	6
‾4	2

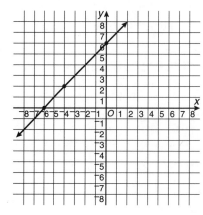

3.

x	y
0	‾2
4	0
8	2

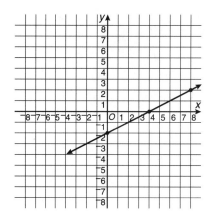

Page 184

1. $\frac{1}{3}$, positive
2. $\frac{7}{2}$, negative
3. $\frac{1}{3}$, negative

Answer Key

Page 185

	a	b	c
1.	$-\frac{1}{3}$	2	$^-1$
2.	2	$-\frac{3}{4}$	$\frac{1}{2}$
3.	$-\frac{6}{5}$	$\frac{5}{9}$	3

Page 186

	a	b	c
1.	>	<	>
2.	>	>	<
3.	<	>	=
4.	=	<	>
5.	true	false	true
6.	false	true	false
7.	false	true	true

Page 187

	a	b	c
1.	$x > 16$	$x \le 15$	$x < 25$
2.	$x \le 7$	$x > 3$	$x \ge 6$
3.	$x > 15$	$x \le 24$	$x > 23$
4.	$x > 24$	$x \ge 25$	$x \ge 35$
5.	$x < {}^-2$	$x \ge {}^-4$	$x < 9$
6.	$x \ge {}^-2$	$x > {}^-8$	$x \le {}^-5$

Page 188

	a	b	c
1.	$x < 20$	$x \ge {}^-16$	$x \le {}^-18$
2.	$x > 5$	$x \ge {}^-5$	$x < 4$
3.	$x < 3$	$x < 7$	$x \le {}^-4$
4.	$x < 6$	$x \ge 7$	$x > 5$
5.	$x \le {}^-5$	$x > {}^-9$	$x > 9$

Page 189

1. 8.5 feet
2. 5 days
3. $2,300
4. $240

Page 191

1. June, December
2. February, April, July, and November
3. November–December
4. June–July
5. January and September
6. 15
7. 55
8. 55

Page 192

1. $-\frac{1}{2}$
2. $x < 35$
3. Tonya is 4.
4. $t \ge 14$
5. 4 days
6. April has a higher rate of growth.
7. (10, 5)
8. No more than $290

Answer Key

Page 193 Unit 8 Review

1. yes, Domain: {⁻1, 1, 2, 3}   Range: {2, 4, 6}
2. no, Domain: {⁻4, 1, 5}   Range: {⁻3, 1, 6, 7}
3. Solutions for the ordered pairs will vary, but the line graphs will be the same.

a.

x	y
0	⁻6
3	0
4	2

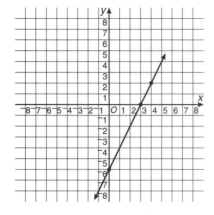

b.

x	y
7	0
5	1
3	2

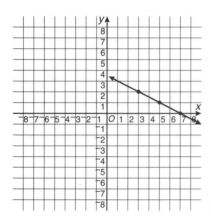

	a	b	c
4.	⁻3	2	⁻1
5.	x > 32	x ≤ 66	x ≥ ⁻5
6.	x < 2	x > 4	x ≥ 2

UNIT 9

Page 194

	a	b	c	d
1.	ray	line	point	line segment

2. a. parallel lines
   b. intersecting lines
   c. perpendicular lines
   d. intersecting lines

Page 195

	a	b	c	d
1.	∠GHI	∠T	∠XYZ	∠ABC
2.	obtuse	straight	acute	right

Page 196

1. a. isosceles
   b. equilateral
   c. isosceles
   d. scalene
2. a. acute
   b. right
   c. obtuse
   d. obtuse

Page 197

1. a. regular
   b. irregular
   c. regular
   d. irregular
2. a. irregular
   b. irregular
   c. regular
   d. irregular
3. a. triangle
   b. quadrilateral
   c. pentagon
   d. octagon
4. a. hexagon
   b. hexagon
   c. pentagon
   d. quadrilateral

Answer Key

Page 198

1. 28.8 centimeters
2. 50 inches
3. 164 meters
4. 0.204 kilometers
5. 22 yards
6. 310 feet

Page 199

1. 44 feet
2. 2 kilometers
3. 232 centimeters
4. 558 centimeters
5. 5.2 kilometers
6. 216 inches

Page 201

1. $270
2. 576 inches
3. 34 meters
4. 980 inches

Page 202

1. 160 square meters
2. 4,567.5 square feet
3. 4,800 square meters
4. 375 square kilometers
5. 17.5 square meters
6. 137.5 square inches

Page 203

1. 55.2 square meters
2. 384 square inches
3. 2,480 square centimeters
4. 300 square meters
5. 150 square meters
6. 2,268 square feet
7. 80 square inches
8. 13.2 square meters

Page 204

1. 550 square inches
2. 72 square yards
3. 85.5 square meters

Page 205

1. 288 square feet
2. 3,050 square centimeters
3. 1,332 square inches
4. $57\frac{1}{4}$ square yards
5. 46 square feet
6. 470 square centimeters
7. 9,400 square inches
8. 18 square feet

Page 206

1. a. 70 square centimeters
   b. 6.75 square meters
   c. 58 square yards
2. a. 2,887.5 square millimeters
   b. 71.76 square feet
   c. 25 square inches

Page 207

	a	b	c
1.	168 sq. m	22.05 sq. yd	459 sq. in.
2.	625 sq. cm	1,950 sq. mm	304 sq. ft
3.	100 square inches		
4.	$21\frac{1}{8}$ square feet		
5.	252 square centimeters		
6.	128 square yards		

Page 208

1. 5.4 cubic meters
2. 343 cubic meters
3. 17,280 cubic feet
4. 189 cubic yards
5. 59,675 cubic centimeters
6. 960 cubic feet
7. 4,104 cubic inches
8. 35 cubic meters

Page 209

1. 21.98 inches
2. 219.8 centimeters
3. 1,099 millimeters
4. 10.99 yards
5. 19.78 meters
6. 143.53 centimeters

Page 210

1. 38.465 square feet
2. 615.44 square inches
3. 38.47 square meters
4. 13.8474 square meters
5. 7 gallons
6. 55.39 square centimeters

Page 211

1. 40.00 cubic yards
2. 2.3079 cubic meters
3. 10.99 cubic inches
4. 1,038.56 cubic meters
5. 67.31 cubic meters
6. 953.78 cubic centimeters

Page 213

1. 5 centimeters
2. 1 foot
3. 4 inches
4. 6 inches
5. 300 square meters
6. 864 square inches
7. 4,800 cubic inches
8. 1,800 cubic inches

Page 214

1. 125 feet
2. 6 meters
3. 10 yards
4. 22 feet
5. 12 inches
6. 12.5 centimeters
7. 120 yards
8. 16 inches

Page 215   Unit 9 Review

	a	b	c	d
1.	right	acute	straight	obtuse
2.	regular	irregular	irregular	regular

3. a. equilateral
   b. scalene
   c. obtuse
   d. right
4. 48,230.4 cubic centimeters
5. 94 square yards
6. 75 square feet
7. 40 inches

UNIT 10

Page 216

	a	b	c
1.	3 ft 3 in.	4 ft 4 in.	1 T 500 lb
2.	2 lb 3 oz	3 lb 12 oz	3 mi 270 yd
3.	8 qt 1 pt	3 pt 1 c	5 gal 1 qt
4.	216 in.	48 in.	10,560 ft
5.	128 oz	192 oz	6,000 lb
6.	29 c	32 c	40 pt

Page 217

	a	b	c
1.	15 m	4 mm	3 km
2.	5 m	20 cm	200 cm
3.	700 cm	150 mm	1,200,000 m
4.	22,500 cm; 225,000 mm	136,000 m	8,400 cm
5.	1.2 m	4.346 km	89 cm
6.	93 cm; 0.93 m	0.750 km	0.11 m

Page 218

	a	b	c
1.	1 g	4 kg	100 kg
2.	500 g	5 kg	20 g
3.	10,000 g	4,800 g	760 g
4.	4 g	1,092 g	305,000 g
5.	0.0028 kg	0.007 kg	3.094 kg
6.	0.925 kg	0.05243 kg	0.061 kg

Answer Key

Page 219

	a	b	c
1.	60 L	750 mL	350 L
2.	300 mL	50 mL	3 L
3.	700 mL	8,000 mL	1,600 mL
4.	421,000 mL	3,090 mL	424 mL
5.	8.883 L	0.3907 L	0.014 L
6.	0.0125 L	0.208 L	0.079 L

Page 220

	a	b
1.	$\frac{1}{3}$	$\frac{1}{7}$
2.	$\frac{1}{2}$	$\frac{1}{2}$
3.	$\frac{1}{4}$	$\frac{4}{5}$
4.	5	$\frac{5}{4}$
5.	$\frac{17}{20}$	$\frac{5}{3}$
6.	1	$\frac{1}{2}$
7.	2	1

Page 221

1. $\frac{1}{9}$
2. $\frac{1}{16}$
3. $\frac{1}{125}$
4. $\frac{27}{64}$
5. $\frac{8}{27}$
6. $\frac{100}{1}$

Page 222

	a	b	c
1.	true	false	true
2.	false	true	true
3.	true	true	false

Page 223

	a	b	c
1.	$x = 20$	$x = 6$	$x = 12$
2.	$x = 27$	$x = 30$	$x = 10$
3.	$x = 3$	$x = 16$	$x = 100$
4.	$x = 21$	$x = 2$	$x = 2$

Page 224

1. $36.10
2. $1.30
3. $4.00
4. $290.40
5. 50 miles
6. $26.25

Page 225

1. 50; 100; 150; 200; 250
2. 20; 40; 60; 80; 100; 120; 140
3. 6; 12; 18; 24; 30; 36; 42

Page 226

	a	b	c	d
1.	YZ; 3	XZ; 4	YZ; 3	XZ; 4

2. a. $\frac{AC}{XZ} = \frac{AB}{XY}, \frac{2}{4} = \frac{1}{2}$

   b. $\frac{BC}{AB} = \frac{YZ}{XY}, \frac{1.5}{1} = \frac{3}{2}$

   c. $\frac{YZ}{BC} = \frac{XZ}{AC}, \frac{3}{1.5} = \frac{4}{2}$

   d. $\frac{XY}{AB} = \frac{XZ}{AC}, \frac{2}{1} = \frac{4}{2}$

3. a. $\frac{XY}{XZ} = \frac{AB}{AC}, \frac{2}{4} = \frac{1}{2}$

   b. $\frac{YZ}{XZ} = \frac{BC}{AC}, \frac{3}{4} = \frac{1.5}{2}$

   c. $\frac{AC}{BC} = \frac{XZ}{YZ}, \frac{2}{1.5} = \frac{4}{3}$

   d. $\frac{AC}{AB} = \frac{XZ}{XY}, \frac{2}{1} = \frac{4}{2}$

Page 227

1. $XY = 21$ in.
2. $XY = 3\frac{2}{3}$ ft
3. $BC = 8$ m
4. $BC = 8$ cm
5. $XY = \frac{1}{2}$ yd
6. $YZ = 2$ ft

Page 228

1. 50 feet tall
2. 555 feet tall
3. 40 feet tall
4. 100 feet tall

Page 229

	a	b	c
1.	$c = 13$	$b = 24$	$c = 5$
2.	$a = 9$	$c = 2$	$b = 8$

Page 231

1. $281.25
2. 72 centimeters long
3. 2,258 people
4. Diane is 15; her brother is 3.
5. Raheem, Richmond; Harold, Brookdale; Katarina, Montague
6. $64.80

Page 232　Unit 10 Review

	a	b	c
1.	0.06	48	0.016
2.	2	10,000	5 ft 6 in.
3.	3000	42,410	5,200

	a	b
4.	$\frac{1}{2}$	$\frac{7}{13}$

	a	b	c
5.	true	false	true
6.	$x = 20$	$x = 10$	$x = 35$

7. 45 minutes
8. 2 inches
9. $\frac{1}{27}$
10. 30 feet

Final Review

Page 233

1. a. 8 thousands
   b. 0 tens
   c. 2 tenths
   d. 6 thousandths

	a	b	c	d
2.	9,554	31,759	466	2,091
3.	864	142,725	26 R1	92

	a	b	c
4.	253	1,713	10,575
5.	8,532	56	41 R1

	a	b	c	d	e
6.	$\frac{2}{5}$	$\frac{3}{2}$	$\frac{1}{3}$	$\frac{14}{3}$	$\frac{3}{25}$

	a	b	c	d
7.	1	$14\frac{1}{10}$	$3\frac{7}{24}$	$\frac{7}{30}$

8. $43\frac{3}{4}$ yards
9. $0.69

Page 234

	a	b	c
10.	10	16	$3\frac{3}{4}$
11.	$1\frac{1}{2}$	$8\frac{1}{4}$	$\frac{3}{2}$

	a	b	c	d
12.	$\frac{3}{10}$	$1\frac{17}{100}$	$\frac{9}{1,000}$	$\frac{1}{100}$
13.	0.8	0.23	0.05	0.008
14.	7.57	69.106	7.27	8.01
15.	117.78	0.9997	0.2475	6.7

	a	b
16.	$0.35 = \frac{7}{20}$	$0.08 = \frac{2}{25}$
17.	20	20%
18.	90	36
19.	$15.75	$85.20

Answer Key

Page 235

	a	b	c	d
20.	$^-2$	11	$^-75$	4

	a	b	c
21.	1	$-\frac{9}{11}$	$^-6$

	a	b	c	d
22.	acute	straight	right	obtuse
23.	regular	irregular	regular	irregular
24.	isosceles	scalene	equilateral	isosceles

25. 54 square meters

26. 120 yards

Page 236

	a	b	c
27.	$(^-3, 9)$	$(1, 1)$	$(4, 5)$
28.	2 gal 2 qt	16 c	650,000 cm
29.	1ft 4 in.	3,000 lb	0.006 L
30.	4,000 g	23 cm	9,000 mL

	a	b	c	d
31.	$x = 22$	$x = 5$	$x = {}^-6$	$x = 10$
32.	$x = 9$	$x = 6$	$x = 14$	$x = 36$
33.	$x = 8$	$x = 6$	$x = 5$	$x = 13$

	a	b
34.	$\frac{7}{12}$	$\frac{1}{8}$

	a	b	c	d
35.	$x \geq 3$	$x > 15$	$x > 3$	$x \geq {}^-40$

36. 8 cm

37. $\frac{1}{3}$

Mastery Test

Teacher's Guide Page 20

1.	D	8.	B
2.	C	9.	B
3.	C	10.	C
4.	A	11.	A
5.	B	12.	B
6.	C	13.	C
7.	D	14.	D

Teacher's Guide Page 21

15.	B	22.	D
16.	B	23.	B
17.	A	24.	C
18.	D	25.	B
19.	A	26.	C
20.	C	27.	D
21.	A	28.	B

Teacher's Guide Page 22

29.	B	37.	C
30.	D	38.	D
31.	A	39.	A
32.	C	40.	B
33.	A	41.	A
34.	A	42.	A
35.	A	43.	D
36.	A	44.	A

Teacher's Guide Page 23

45.	D	51.	D
46.	C	52.	C
47.	A	53.	C
48.	C	54.	A
49.	D	55.	D
50.	A	56.	B

Teacher's Guide Page 24

57.	D	64.	B
58.	A	65.	A
59.	A	66.	B
60.	D	67.	D
61.	D	68.	C
62.	B	69.	B
63.	A	70.	A